PROJECTS / PROCESSES
VOLUME IV

Explorations of the Contemporary

PROJECTS / PROCESSES VOLUME IV

Explorations of the Contemporary

Series Editor: Senjuti Mukherjee

HARPER DESIGN
An Imprint of HarperCollinsPublishers

First published in India in 2019 by
HarperCollins *Publishers*
A-75, Sector 57, Noida, Uttar Pradesh 201301, India
www.harpercollins.co.in

2 4 6 8 10 9 7 5 3 1

P-ISBN: 978-93-5357-533-5

Typeset in 9/14.2 Freight at
Serendipity Arts Foundation

Printed and bound at
Replika Press Pvt. Ltd.

Contents

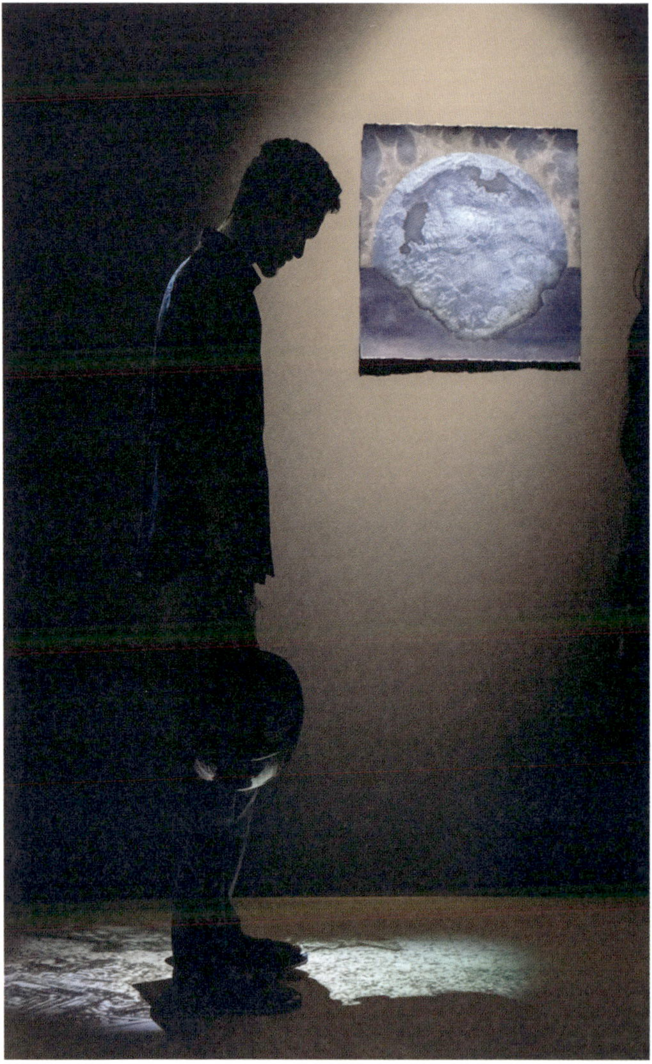

Notes from Emptiness (2018); Jagrut Raval

Dharti Arts Residency A Serendipity Arts Foundation initiative

Venue Old Goa Institute of Management

Dharti Arts Residency

A Serendipity Arts Foundation initiative
Critic-in-residence *Kamayani Sharma*
Programme Designer *Gayatri Uppal*
Artists *Jagrut Raval, Khushbu Patel, Pannaga Jois and Ravi Kumar Chaurasiya*

Dharti Arts Residency is a three-month artists' residency based in New Delhi. Conceptualised as an intensive, studio-based residency for emerging artists, Dharti provides its residents space and resources to develop their practice, work on a new project, and interact with the broader art community in the city. The residency is held annually between the months of May and August.

In the course of the three months, the four artists selected for the programme participate in a lineup of peer-to-peer conversations, critique sessions, gallery and studio visits, artist talks and presentations etc. Alongside, they will be required to conceptualise and produce a new work. The residency concludes with a week-long open studio.

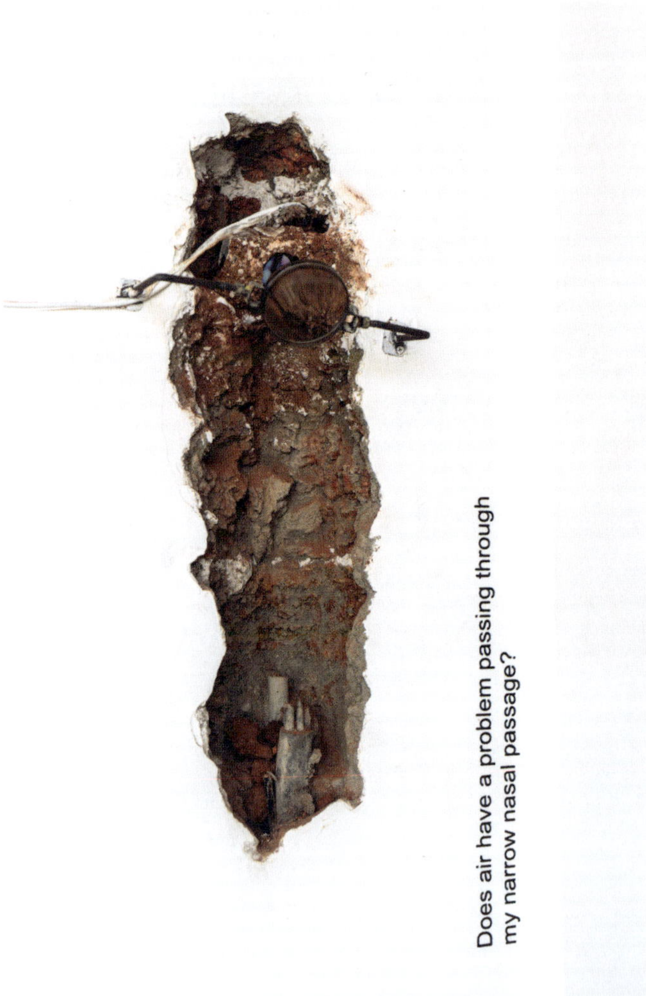

Breaking Opacity in Micro Pieces (2018); Khushbu Patel

Loving with Language: Reflections on Writing Alongside Art

KAMAYANI SHARMA

I.

The Internet is acerbic. There exists a website that has been set up to generate random "art criticism" quotes in response to any five-digit number.

http://www.pixmaven.com/phrase_generator.html[1]

The sentences spewed out by the algorithm are expectedly pretentious; an obvious joke about the opacity of language that often plagues its own use in the serious discussion of art. It's funny because it's true.

II.

A scene in *Velvet Buzzsaw* (2019), a film satirising the horrors of the art world, features a conversation between an art enthusiast and icy critic Morf Vandewalt:

> "I heard he was crushed."
>
> "By the car?"
>
> "Your review."[2]

It's a telling depiction, one tapping into a stock characterisation, inadvertently echoed by the term "critic-in-residence," as if one were talking about a disapproving, verbose parent, waiting at the dinner table to find faults in the art made in the course of the day. The reality is a lot less contentious. When I took up the role of critic for the Dharti Arts Residency at Serendipity Arts Foundation in the summer of 2018 it was with an interest in reordering my relationship with art. Instead of encountering finished or resolved artworks in a controlled setting—a gallery or museum—I was keen to respond to the often-messy processes they entailed, in the studio.

*

There is a lure to experiencing the unfolding of someone else's art, seeing it transform from a thought to a physical thing. It's a lure similar to the heady promise of the present tense, a temporal register in which the writer tracks events, converting the world into text as it happens, walking the length of sentences to discover how they might end.

My reflections on writing about art that was yet to be created were nourished by those of Grant Kester. He considers the role of criticism in relation to now-ubiquitous "dialogical" social art practices, which are characterised by collaboration, extended duration, simultaneity of production and reception and a lack of predictability about their final form. One of his chief concerns, most relevant to mine during Dharti, is the nature of the conversation between the physical effects of the work and its abstract appeal. Kester's argument in favour of a mutually illuminating dynamic of actual processes and conceptual frames resonated with me. Dialogue becomes a governing principle in a residency space where the critic is present. The shot/reverse-shot model of conventional criticism (recognisable from film scenes in which two characters have a conversation), based on the spatiotemporal gap between the moment of exhibition and that of critique, doesn't apply to the residency.

"When does the work begin and when does it end? What are the boundaries of the field within which it operates, and how were they determined? At the most basic level, can we even agree as to what constitutes the object of criticism? Because we are dealing with an unfolding process, rather than, or in addition to, a discrete image, object, or event defined by set limits of space (the walls of a gallery) or time (the duration of a performance or commission), these questions become decisive in the analysis of the work."[3]

III.

What are the modes of engagement possible for a critic during a three-month tenure of witnessing the synthesis of art?

Art writing is a broad umbrella, under which criticism huddles. No doubt there is a smattering of opportunity for publication in niche magazines and news outlets but at least in South Asia, the writing itself is often limited to the reportorial, without a strong evaluative component. Perhaps that's because a dedicated reading public is comparatively scant. Within the art world itself, unprotected by the distance necessary for assessment, the art writer cannot be a judge and is often an accomplice. Within this insular sphere, two ready options seem to be: that of a curator or that of a catalogue contributor. Let us consider them, briefly.

The word "curator" comes from the Latin word meaning "to care"; it has an ecclesiastical ancestry, originally signifying a member of the clergy who tended to souls. In its secular sense, it broadly refers to a person who either preserves cultural artefacts or organises exhibitions, developing a proposition and choosing works that speak to it. Girish Shahane has argued that contemporary curators, while powerful in the global market of biennales and blockbuster shows, have become invested in the non-aesthetic claims of art—moral or political, for example—rather than its phenomenal, autonomous qualities. Often the emphasis on the ideas behind the art reveals a commitment to ideology at the expense of "the sensible."[4]

"... what has always attracted people to art, and continues to do so, is precisely what critics focus upon, and curators, at least in their writing, frequently ignore: the relationship, irreducible and untranslatable bond, formed between artwork and spectator in the act of viewing."[5]

This "writing" which he playfully calls "curatorspeak" is informed by declarative statements in theor-ese[6] meant to demonstrate the value of art as mainly a sociopolitical function rather than an expressive one.

Kester supports Shahane's thesis when he points out how much contemporary criticism has become absurdly formulaic, furnishing a sort of mathematical "proof" of what the art is "supposed" to do, rather than its actual effects on the viewer.[7] In the Euro-American context it has been suggested that this has to do with the turn towards conceptual art. In India, over the past couple of decades and particularly with the growth of the art market in the mid-2000s, there has been a tendency to "legitimise" writing on art for a global viewership through obscurantist text. Usually glimpsed on the walls of galleries, this is the sort of writing that Internet generators lampoon.

This brings me to the second choice of role for the critic in a residency: that of a catalogue contributor.

Besides curators, influential art writers—this includes critics and historians—frequently pen essays for exhibitions in well-known galleries and museums. Having written my share of term papers, I can attest to the academic slant that invariably creeps into this genre of art writing, a close cousin of curatorspeak. There is often a fervent need to explain the works, the writer resorting to a deductive exercise—premise 1- premise 2-conclusion—meant to reveal everything to a presumably clueless reader.

This manages a hat-trick of pedantry: it robs the artwork of its autonomy, subordinates the language of the artist to that of the writer, and infantilises the spectator-reader seeing the work and perhaps engaging with the discourse around it. Sure, usually some explanation is welcome, especially for viewers and readers who may not be conversant with art history, but ironically, this is accomplished in a language so rooted in its dense, theoretical habitat that it is unable to be grafted into a wider readership. The language of these essays is frequently larded with gatekeeping jargon, causing it to congeal around the art objects and rendering them invisible.

I reject both these positions, of curator and catalogue essayist.

IV.

I am not a curator—I was neither involved in the selection of artists nor can I say that I played a noteworthy role in deciding how the exhibition would be mounted. Jagrut Raval, Khushbu Patel, Pannaga Jois and Ravi Kumar Chaurasiya are all artists with an astute understanding of their relationships to the mediums they work with, as well as the questions they want to ask.

On the opening night of the residency's Open Studio in Delhi, someone compared my involvement with the artists-in-residence to that of an editor. This is a descriptor I am more comfortable with, given that I have both helped edit an art magazine and, as a writer, had the good fortune of working with some excellent editors. Over the course of the three months in which I interacted with the artists at Dharti, meeting them at least once a week for long and thorough discussions, I tried to understand their intentions and gave extensive responses. I suggested tweaks, shared readings and lookings (yes, it should be a word in our line of work, the consumption of images is central) and spent a lot of time asking questions and hearing them out. There are less rewarding aspects to editing that have nothing to do with the people and everything to do with the nature of the craft—it can seem thankless as one's labour might be rendered invisible, effaced before the masterpiece (one hopes!) one has contributed to. This is in no way similar to the "star status" of the curator.

But, ironically, also in this sense, the spirit of what I was doing at Dharti was close to the way in which Hans Ulrich Obrist talks about the role of the curator as an enabler.[8] It's a word that gets pejoratively used these days for those who encourage self-destructive habits, and I facetiously mention this because art can be one too. But since the Dharti studio was not a den of vice, I'll stick to my original use of the word, as someone who supports and helps. It's a quasi-therapeutic dynamic, in that there is a lot of listening and imagining of what's going on in another person's mind.

But as much as I would indulge that metaphor, I also resist it. In doing so, I reject the abstruse approach of the theoriser. I'm thinking of Susan Sontag's eloquent repudiation of the brute interpretive strategies that Freudian psychoanalysis exemplified: " as it excavates, it destroys; it digs 'behind' the text, to find a subtext which is the true one."[9] This is akin to the rough handling of the art object, in the way it masquerades as donnish attention in the catalogue essay that has all of the curator's spiel and none of their care. In fact, the conversation that should be occurring between the artwork and the viewer is now taking place between the curator/theoriser and critic.

The relationship of love between art and art enthusiast seems to be missing.

I mean love not in the sense of naïve applause but in the deeper sense of attention and care, which does not preclude opinion, even a harsh one. After all, part of love is unflinching candour and authenticity of response.

V.

> "... acts of criticism which would supply really accurate, sharp, loving description of the appearance of a work of art ...we need an erotics of art."[10]
>
> - Susan Sontag, *Against Interpretation*, Part I

The four artists have distinct practices unbound by any framework, and I, choosing to be neither curator nor theoriser, cannot superimpose one on the exhibition. Thus, I must define for myself my task as critic in this specific context, but it mimics the external conditions I have elucidated before.

The question is twofold:

1. In the absence of a curatorial proposition, what is at stake?
i.e.
Why write?
2. What alternative forms can a critical essay take?
i.e.
How to write?

I ask the first question keeping in mind Geeta Kapur's essay for the seminal 1981 exhibition, *Place for People*.[11] A survey of abstraction against which the "repressed" strand of narrative Indian art was staged, Kapur's piece acquired the status of a manifesto from a vantage point decades after the moment. Why I bring that specific show up is also because Kapur too disagreed with being characterised as a curator, stating that she was part of the exhibiting group, "the seventh member," she reiterated in a conversation in August 2018.[12]

But unlike the sense of community and ideological affinity that spawned that landmark show, a residency space to which strangers are invited cannot establish relations among participants in such a manner. There is no graph to plot coordinates on; the ground is of a different texture, and the figures disparate. No uniting force exists to artificially structure the show. Further, it needn't be retrofitted with one to derive meaning like some hermeneutic ninja manoeuvre.

Perhaps testament to its vintage, I returned to Sontag's notion of erotics while making my notes and doing my research. At one level, it is compatible with Kester and Shahane's encouragement to attend to the artwork qua itself, before launching into language. On another, it was a felicitous method for the companionate position I had taken up vis-à-vis the artists.

With this in mind, the programme that I created for myself was spread out over two phases: the first was the three-month period of the residency during which I witnessed the artists' processes, and the second was the four months of actually drafting the essays. The chief challenge was developing an approach that would allow me to remain authentic to the artists' vision but also avoid ventriloquism. In order to develop a text that was both record and interpretation, I had to imagine it as a transversal line slicing two parallel ones: the artists and the future spectator-readers. This would allow the essay to have a relationship with both parties while retaining its independence as a piece of writing in its own right.

Love became a vector along which I tried to plot the transversal.

VI.

> "(to write on something is to outmode it.)"[13]
> - Roland Barthes, *A Lover's Discourse*, 98

In the contemporary scenario, when the connection between art objects and words is tenuous and unconvincing, how can language intervene, acknowledge the loving gaze and effect the mediation?

Rosalind Krauss, doyenne of the very tendency Kester opposes (and this opposition can be a moment of productive agonism), calls this sort of Barthesian move "paraliterary." It "simply cannot be called criticism but it cannot for that matter be called not-criticism either. Rather criticism finds itself in a dramatic web of many voices, citations, asides, divigations."[14]

The form of the zine became a template because of its collage-like aesthetic that allowed for a range of elements to be orchestrated on one plane with equal importance. Different categories of texts and images could be excerpted, cited and assembled in one place. This approach let me facilitate conversations between various registers, rhetorical flexes and inspirations that were guiding the artists.

I wove into each essay fragments of conversations, visual and literary references that had informed their work and images of the work-in-progress to challenge the top-down strategy of imposing onto finished works a vocabulary not tailored for it. Over these I tried to spread a cobweb of philosophical and historical analysis, the material of criticism, allowing the artworks to catch the light filtered in through the gossamer, directing the spectator-reader's gaze.

Thus, the Dharti essays were representational in that they indexed the actual artistic process leading to the works—the conversations and labour—while exceeding the limits of the representational to become commentaries on the works themselves. In this sense, the essays were both mimetic and hermeneutic: a translation of the exhibition as well as its exegesis.

While on the topic of translation, I find that much of my work consists of "translating" from one medium to another. The former is variable (paintings, photographs, sculptures, videos etc., all of which were part of the Dharti exhibition) but the latter is always the same: language. The zine aesthetic offered a more "expanded field"[15] for language: annotated, highlighted excerpts, photographs, screenshots of websites, diagrams and scribbles, bits of verse and prose opened up the essay to multimedial, cross-genre possibilities, retaining substantive density while leavening language.

In relation to this, a category of poetics that I found particularly useful was that of ekphrasis, usually defined as "verbal representation of a visual representation."[16] It is an ancient element in art writing, since description is so central to the act. Through these essays, I attempted to test the limits of what ekphrasis could do as a function of critical practice, and discovering its ambivalent, intermedial potential to transport meaning from one mode of representation to others. Going forward, I am interested in exploring further what W. J. T Mitchell has called "ekphrastic hope": "The estrangement of the image/text division is overcome, and a sutured, synthetic form, a verbal icon or imagetext, arises in its place."[17] The Dharti essays are gestures towards eventually achieving, in my writing, a sort of digital ekphrasis: a hypertextual incarnation of the artistic process and critical commentary.

VII.

Sontag's plea for erotics is realised in Barthes' gnomic treatise on the plot of love. Its fragmentary, loose, sinewy format suggests what it's possible to do with a work of criticism that collapses the difference between the surface and the core—between text and subtext. The meanings are not hidden underneath a layer but darkened by shadows; critical language then becomes light, a benign technology of knowledge, not a spade or pickaxe, some violent instrument. Form and content become deliciously inextricable in *A Lover's Discourse*, making it a program for critical writing that is enduring—conceptually dense and light as poetry.

> *"I am both too big and too weak for writing, I am alongside it."*[18]
> - Roland Barthes, A Lover's Discourse, 98

VIII.

> *"The paintings were perfectly at ease. I had fallen in love and I had no language."*[19]
> - Jeanette Winterson, *Art Objects*

During the residency, we read together Jeanette Winterson's essay "Art Objects." The title is a pun on the dual meaning of object-as-thing (*res* in Latin) and object-"as-to oppose." In the first sense,

Winterson conceives of "the art object as an art process, the thing in being." Closer to the commonly understood meaning of in medias res, this gives us the possibility of regarding viewing as a productive interruption—a way of catching the artist in the act, the exhibition as a moment in an ongoing process.

The final exhibition mounted at the Serendipity Festival show is the culmination of a period of many months of work during the residency, and follows years of thinking and making before it. In the second sense, Winterson imagines how art objects to the viewer as she unpacks the experience of being amidst artworks—in medias res as literally being "in the middle of things." Art resists the determinism of an evolutionary theory of life, it "objects to the lie against life, against the spirit" and in that sense, she states, it is like love. We may not live for the purpose of appreciating beauty but, as with falling in love, it makes life worth living.

This thought encapsulates the critical approach to the final exhibition. It is the rhyming of art with love that makes aesthetic objects meaningful, even when we don't quite understand them. Being affected by the artworks and coaxing them to speak for themselves has an erotic charge.

The critical task is to witness the conversation between the spectator and the works as they reveal themselves to each other. Of this, the essay is the record.

But the adventure is finally the viewer's—intimate and transformative.

Notes

[1] "The Instant Art Critique Phrase Generator," Pixmaven, accessed September 10, 2018, http://www.pixmaven.com/phrase_generator.html.

[2] *Velvet Buzzsaw*, directed by Dan Gilroy (2019, Netflix and Dease Pictures Inc; https://www.netflix.com/title/80199689).

[3] Grant Kester, "The Device Laid Bare: On Some Limitations in Current Art Criticism," *e-flux* 50 (December 2013), https://www.e-flux.com/journal/50/59990/the-device-laid-bare-on-some-limitations-in-current-art-criticism/

[4] Duncan Thomas, "The Politics of Art: An interview with Jacques Rancière," *Verso*, November 9, 2015, https://www.versobooks.com/blogs/2320-the-politics-of-art-an-interview-with-jacques-ranciere

[5] Girish Shahane, "Curatorism: In Praise of Folly," *Art India* 17, no. 2 (2012-2013): 33.

[6] I use the word "theor-ese" to mean language that is larded with critical theory terminology without necessarily benefitting the point being made.

[7] Kester, "The Device Laid Bare: On Some Limitations in Current Art Criticism."

[8] Hans Ulrich Obrist, "Hans Ulrich Obrist: the art of curation," *The Guardian*, March 23, 2014, https://www.theguardian.com/artanddesign/2014/mar/23/hans-ulrich-obrist-art-curator

[9] Susan Sontag, "Against Interpretation," in *Against Interpretation and Other Essays* (New York: Picador, 2013), Part I.

[10] Sontag, "Against Interpretation."

[11] Geeta Kapur, Place for People, 1981. Published following the

exhibition *Place for People* at the Rabindra Bhavan, New Delhi and Jehangir Art Gallery, Bombay.

[12] Natasha Ginwala, "Geeta Kapur: On the Curatorial in India," *Afterall*, October 3, 2011, https://www.afterall.org/online/geeta-kapur-on-the-curatorial-in-india-part2#.XJ8fTaavqRs.

[13] Roland Barthes, *A Lover's Discourse: Fragments*, trans. Richard Howard (New York: Hill and Wang, 1978), 98.

[14] Rosalind Krauss, "Poststructuralism and the Paraliterary," October 13 (1980): 37.

[15] Travis Jeppessen, "Hans Ulrich Obrist in Conversation About Inventing New Languages," *Sleek*, December 2, 2016, https://www.sleek-mag.com/article/hans-ulrich-obrist-zhang-jeppesen-miralda/.

[16] James A.W. Heffernan, *Museum of Words: The Poetics of Ekphrasis from Homer to Ashbery* (Chicago: University of Chicago Press, 1994), 3.

[17] W. J. T. Mitchell, "Ekphrasis and the Other," in *Picture Theory: Essays on Verbal and Visual Representation* (Chicago: University of Chicago Press, 1994), 154.

[18] Barthes, *A Lover's Discourse*, 98.

[19] Jeanette Winterson, "Art Objects," in *Art Objects: Essays on Ecstasy and Effrontery* (London: Jonathan Cape, 1995).

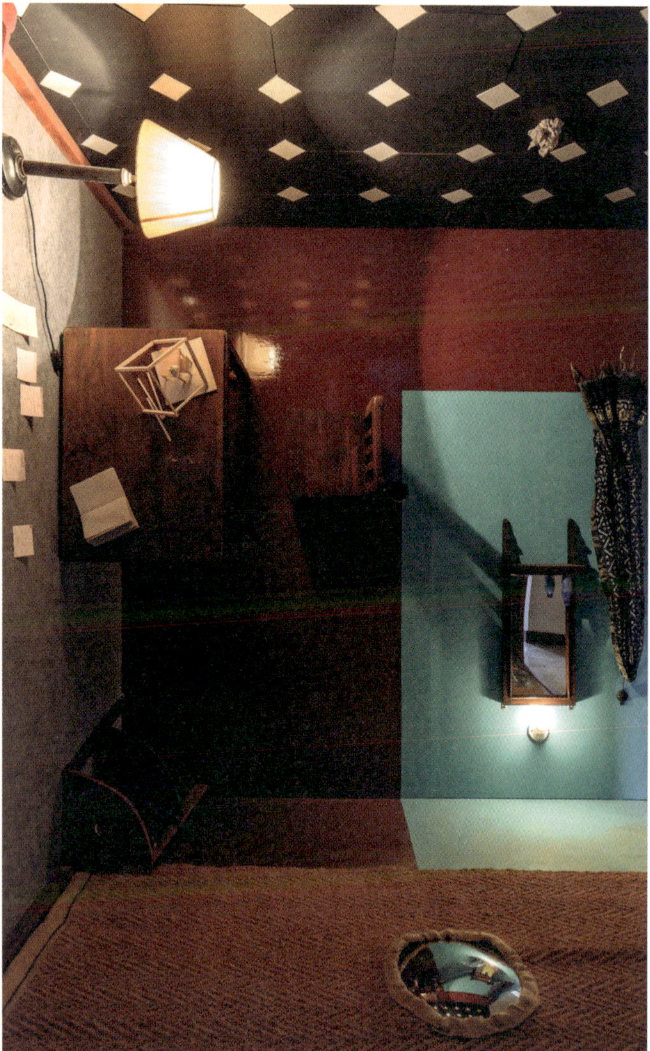

The Persistence of Memory (2018); Pannaga Jois; This performance installation was developed based on the artist's personal retrospection of life triggered by the nature of the studio space at C340, Defence Colony, in New Delhi where she was in-residence at Dharti.

Dharti Arts Residency | 2018

Participating Artists: *Pannaga Jois, Ravi Kumar Chaurasiya, Khushbu Patel, Jagrut Raval*

A review by *Kamayani Sharma*, **Critic-in-residence at Dharti, 2018**

Excerpted from a digital zine. For complete text, refer to URL: https://www.serendipityartsfestival.com/archives-2018//wp-content/uploads/2018/12/Dharti-Arts-Residency-Serendipity-Arts-Foundatin.pdf

PANNAGA JOIS
Persistence of Memory: *Setting the Stage*

If memories were rooms, what would they look like? That's the question Pannaga Jois wants to ask. Over the period of the residency, she spent all her studio time inside a cuboid frame, building a habitat each week, and then turning that surface from a floor into a wall and the ceiling. This Rubik choreography of space and body has been compressed into a time-lapse video displayed alongside the room. I struggled with selecting *The Poetics of Space* by Gaston Bachelard as a reference for the exhibition because it seems so obvious, but it is impossible to avoid the text. In fact, the first chapter is so perspicuous that in its entirety, it would make for an excellent accompaniment to her work. A sample of extracts:

> the house is not experienced from day to day only, on the thread of a narrative, or in the telling of our own story. Through dreams, the various dwelling-places in our lives co-penetrate and retain the treasures of former days. And after we are in the new house, when memories of other places we have lived in come back to us, we travel to the

> lar daydream were acquired there. The house, the bedroom, the garret in which we were alone, furnished the framework for an interminable dream, one that poetry alone, through the creation of a poetic work, could succeed in achieving completely. If we give their function of shelter

> proaching the immemorial. But in the daydream itself, the recollection of moments of confined, simple, shut-in space are experiences of heartwarming space, of a space that does not seek to become extended, but would like above all still to be possessed. In the past, the attic may have

> For the real houses of memory, the houses to which we return in dreams, the houses that are rich in unalterable oneirism, do not readily lend themselves to description.

Images above: Screenshots of excerpts from Gaston Bachelard, *The Poetics of Space*, trans. Maria Jolas (Beacon Press, 1994).

Jois' training in theatrical design formed the basis for her interest in the architectonic aspects of performance and the way in which bodies of performers and spectators relate to place. At the beginning of the residency, she wished to learn architectural modelling so that she could replicate the neighbourhoods of old Delhi and design a performance around people navigating the area. We discussed premodern maps and their techniques of rendering topographies that had less to do with scientific accuracy and more to do with the phenomenology of traversing a known territory.

Jois spent a lot of time building, commissioning or shopping in the markets of Chandni Chowk and Kotla Mubarakpur, and much of her artistry can be read as assemblage. Materials, textures, surfaces and colours—she organised these as if putting together the costumes and props for a play without a script, an endless improvisation, life synthesised into the spatial and temporal confines of a performance piece. Boundaries were blurred between the lineages the work drew on—installation, performance and proscenium theatre.

Claire Bishop points out how installation art has always been difficult to define, because of its inherent intermediality as “any arrangement of objects.”[1] She makes a case for analysing the genre in terms of the experience of the viewing subject:

> The argument, then, is that installation art presupposes a viewing subject who physically enters into the work to experience it, and that it is possible to categorise works of installation by the type of experience that they structure for the viewer. Of course, it is possible to say that all art presumes a subject – insofar as it is *made* by a subject (the artist) and is *received* by a subject (the viewer). In the case

Image above: Screenshot of an excerpt from Claire Bishop, “Installation Art,” *Tate*, Issue 3 (Spring 2005).

In doing so, Bishop also argues that the body, rather than the gaze, of the viewing subject becomes the locus of the artwork, presenting itself to the sensory conditions of the artwork and reanimating it through physical presence and movement. In Jois’ artwork Persistence of Memory, the viewer rehearses the drama of Jois’ “having been there.”

This focus on the body has a specific trajectory in postmodern and feminist aesthetic history. It is a challenge to the masculinist perspective that centred the spectator and emphasises the materiality of the encounter between her and the art object, the registers of the tactile as important as those of the optical.

Gil Perry in *Playing at Home: The House in Contemporary Art* draws attention to installation art’s imbrication with the modernism of women—from Griselda Pollock’s “spaces of femininity” to Miriam Schapiro and Melissa Meyer’s coinage of the term “femmage.”[2]

Is performance only that which occurs when both actor and spectator

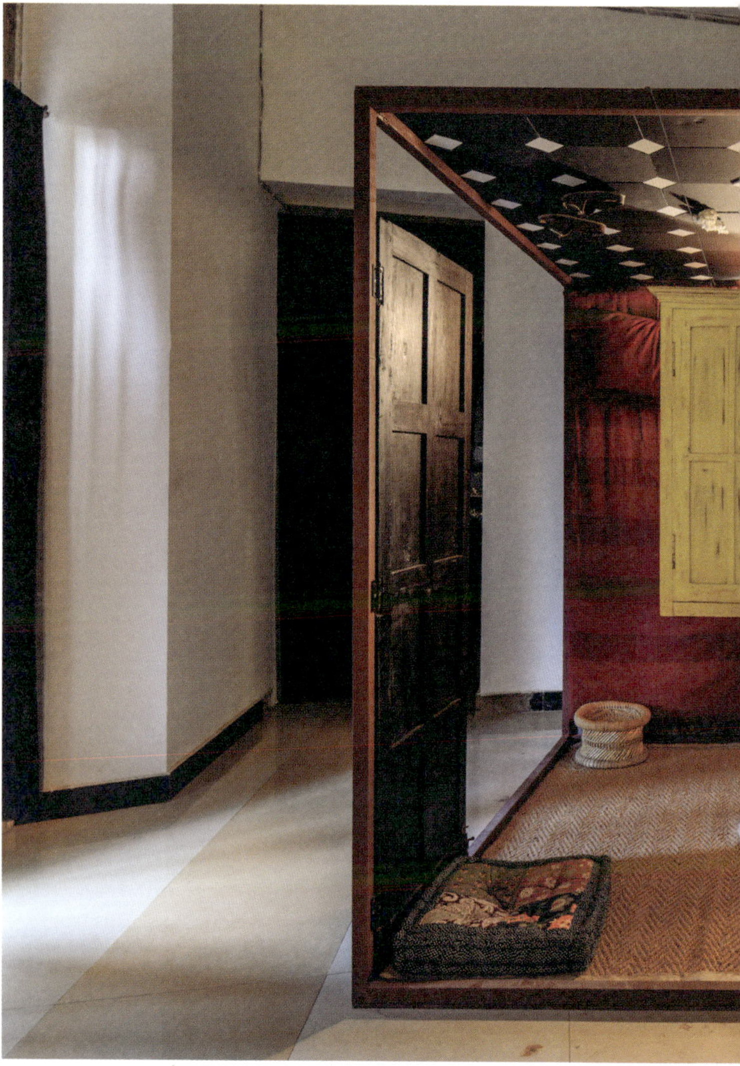

The Persistence of Memory (2018); Pannaga Jois

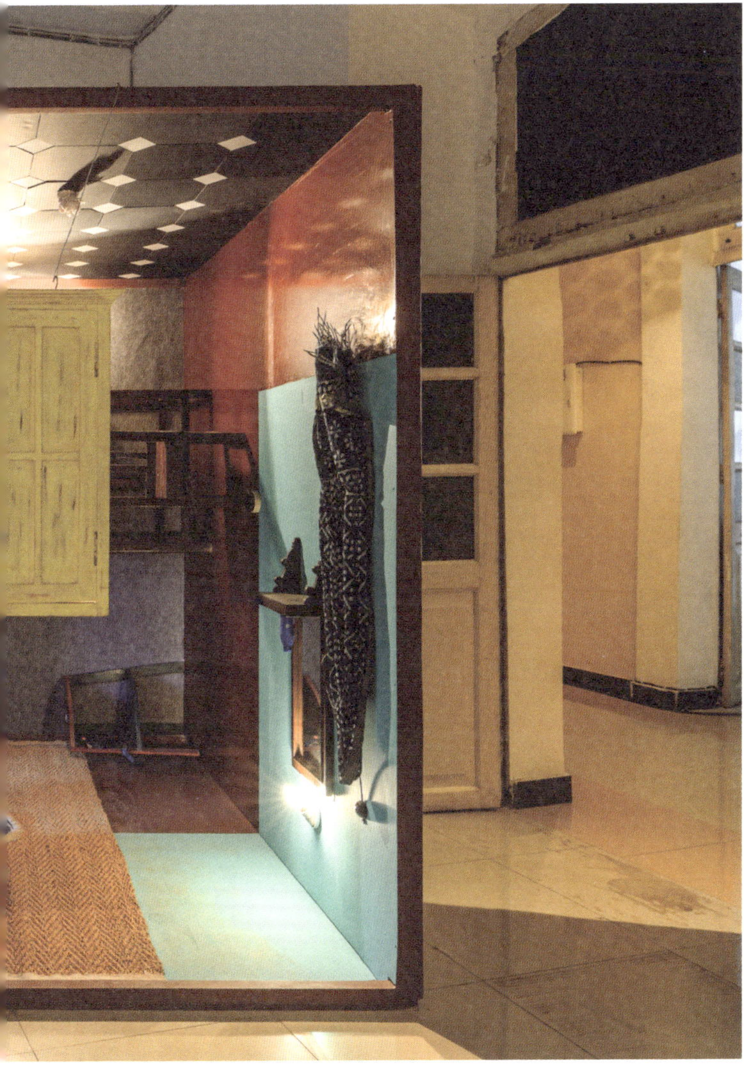

co-exist in the same time and space? Or can the term "performance" accommodate the spatiotemporal delay and distance made possible by contemporary technologies like digital video? A work like Jois' presents an edited version of a past performance alongside the space she constructed and resided in—all of which constitute the total performance. The video and the performance are not exactly discrete elements separated by a gap but recursively cite each other. Whether it's the shoes tacked to the ceiling or the video loop summarising Jois' presence inside the house, or the house standing in for the performance—the work can be read as a relay system of metonymic proofs, parts standing in for wholes, establishing the performance. There is no "liveness," and yet the existence of a performance (separated from life through the ritual of architectural transformations) cannot be denied as one stands before the screen or beholds the used things sticking out of walls inside the cube.

Is the evocation of the performance, the same as nostalgia for old rooms and shelves, part of the performance? A performance within a performance? The sharing of memory becomes a performance, in which the involvement of the spectator is crucial—as voyeur viewing a recording, unseen by the performer, or as witness to the scene of the actual performance. One view of performance is that it is defined not by physical co-presence but quality of engagement. Jois seems to agree with this understanding of video-performance that focuses on the involvement of the spectator. She quotes Peter Brook to me when discussing her work: "I can take any empty space and call it a bare stage. A man walks across this empty space whilst someone else is watching him, and this is all that is needed for an act of theatre to be engaged." One of the books Jois took with her during her stint inside the cube was a collection of Julio Cortazar's short stories, headlined by his most famous one, *BlowUp* (1964). In the story, a photographer observing a couple and taking their pictures realised, upon enlarging them (the "blow-up" of the title), that he has completely misread the drama happening before his eyes: "... that gloomy operation of comparing the memory with the gone reality, a frozen memory..."[3]

In her controversial essay, "Video: The Aesthetics of Narcissism," Rosalind Krauss states that the ontology of video is psychological rather than physical. She compares the nature of video to that of the mirror, "capable of recording and transmitting at the same time... the performing artist is centred between two machines... the camera; the second is the monitor, which re-projects the performer's image with the immediacy of the mirror."[4] I want to extend the possibility of thinking about the spectator as integral to the performance of Jois' work because it involves them traversing the actual site of the performance. The spatialisation of memory allows for the "restaging" of an experience. The spectator becomes the performer.

RAVI KUMAR CHAURASIYA
Techno Rubble

One of the prominent aspects of Ravi Chaurasiya's time at Dharti was the time he spent on research. It made sense to excerpt from a work about the political economy of technological trash, partly because his process seemed to be fuelled by a similar quasi-sociological impulse. During his first presentation, Chaurasiya showed the work he had done as a student in Varanasi; his canvases were full of people and dogs, both dead and alive, dwarfed by garbage dumps. Large in size and made up of multiple panels in some cases, his paintings suggested an ambition and scale that exceeded the frame. Indeed, when he began his residency at Dharti, he was keen to expand his practice. He told me that he had achieved a certain level of satisfaction with his relationship to painting, an ease with technique that had prepared the ground for him to move to other media. In the initial period of the residency, when the artists were trying out a bunch of ideas, Chaurasiya expressed his interest in exploring the problem of waste: "I am planning to work on Garbage in the City. This work series focuses on the population and pollution of the world has reached a crescendo which depicts as if it is a pile of garbage. I would like to present its cons which are affecting our human lives."

This prompted an interrogation of what the word entails. There are many different genres of waste, depending on the materials used and the life-cycle of the objects they are used to make. Also inherent in these discussions was Chaurasiya's attempt to figure out a method to approach a sensitive subject like this. In India, the management of waste is a highly political issue because of the existence of an oppressive caste system that forces certain communities into manual scavenging and waste picking. The issue of waste management has become particularly charged in the context of the current government's attempts to co-opt the language of civic sanitation through programs like Swachh Bharat. Focussing on a middle-class electorate's desire for "clean" urban spaces, the state is subtly abdicating responsibility for the labour doing the work. For Chaurasiya, the main point of interest in the problem of garbage was the environmental impact it has on society and the planet. During his time at the residency, he engaged with various analyses of the contemporary situation and reflected on the way in which the problem of ecological disaster was the result of an inherently violent logic of organising all kinds of relations—between humans, between humans and their surroundings, and between humans and the things they produce and consume.

His initial forays into the problem of non-degradable materials polluting the world were in the vein of a concerned citizen, curious about the circuits and chains that transformed objects from items of utility to discarded junk. Any understanding of the phenomenon of garbage would be impossible without an understanding of the economy. Following group sessions during the first month at Dharti, Chaurasiya narrowed the scope of his research to the category of electronic waste.

This is a particularly egregious variety of waste because it epitomises everything that is wrong with neo-liberalism—global inequities between the developed world and the developing one. In the case of e-waste, the toxic substances used to make them, and the expense of disposing them, have become reasons for the wealthiest countries to

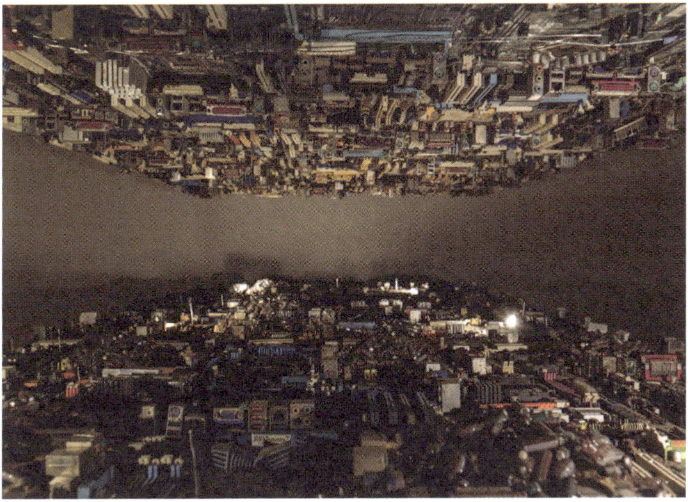

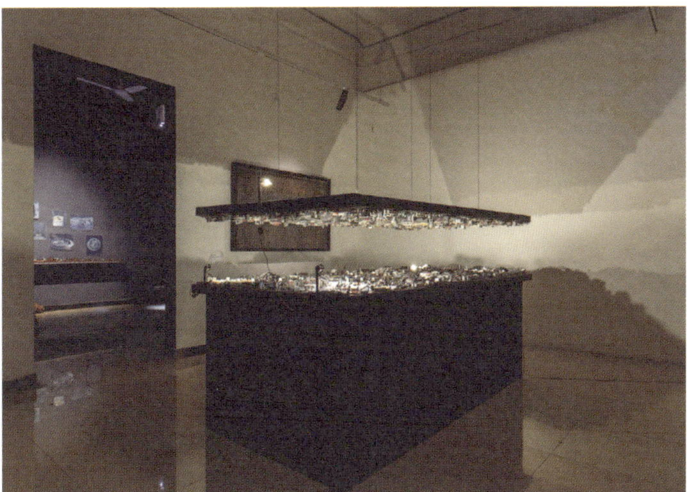

The City of E-Waste (2018); Ravi Kumar Chaurasiya;
Computer motherboard, electronic scrap, plaster of Paris, ply board, sound, artwork; 96 x 48 x 60 inches

turn some of the poorest ones into dumping grounds. It is hard not to think of the trash-filled dystopia film like *Wall-E* (2008) as an allegory for this sort of exploitative regime.

The questions that Chaurasiya seems to be asking are: What is the status of stuff? What fantasies do we spin about things? What does it even mean to discard something in a world overrun with immortal, toxic material? Crucial to this is the economic analysis in which these systems exist, as a way of comprehending the wider context in which capital moved, reproduced, digested and then excreted what it could not absorb. The metaphor of biological processes is not without reason. One of the leading Marxist scholars on ecology, John Bellamy Foster has recouped Karl Marx's idea of the "metabolic rift" to mount an exegesis of the way in which the human-environment dynamic has suffered under late capitalism.[5] If we take the definition of metabolism to be chemical processes that occur within an organism in order to maintain life, then we can begin to see how Marx worked out his idea of "Stoffwechsel" or metabolism as a response to developments in nineteenth century agricultural chemistry, particularly the problem of soil depletion.

In the twentieth century discourse of critical ecology, which includes contemporary notions of the anthropocene and the conversation around climate change, the idea of a "metabolic rift" between humans and the planet they occupy is an analytically rich one. In particular, it offers a lens to study the way in which the scaling up of industry and its conversion into finance capital has further alienated labour from life-worlds, and deepened the gap between use-value (the utility of things) and exchange-value (their monetary price).

India contributes 12% of the world's e-waste production and recycles less than 2% of this. Getting in touch with the NGO Chintan, Chaurasiya spent many days of his research time in visiting Seelampur, one of North India's biggest e-waste dumps. It's a site which represents the dark underbelly of India's digital industry—a place where old technology goes to be reincarnated, used phones and computers taken apart and sold to scrap dealers, valuable metals extracted from motherboards, microchips, circuit boards and batteries, and sold to smelting plants and chemical-based industries.

Chaurasiya used all the scrap or reusable material in an installation titled *The City of E-Waste*, and to subtler effect in the *Dump Yard* series of mixed-media paintings. Chaurasiya's bleak, brown-toned canvases and hardware bricolage bring to mind the material churn of the fictional city of Leonia in Italo Calvino's *Invisible Cities*:

> **wider perimeter. Besides, the more Leonia's talent for making new materials excels, the more the rubbish improves in quality, resists time, the elements, fermentations, combustions. A fortress of indestructible leftovers surrounds Leonia, dominating it on every side, like a chain of mountains.**
>
> **This is the result: the more Leonia expels goods, the more it accumulates them; the scales of its past are soldered into a cuirass that cannot be removed. As the city is renewed each day, it preserves all of itself in its only definitive form: yesterday's sweepings piled up on the sweepings of the day before yesterday and of all its days and years and decades.**

Image above: Screenshot of an excerpt from Italo Calvino, *Invisible Cities*, trans. by William Weaver (Harcourt Brace & Company, 1974).

One of the problems of repurposing refuse or drawing on its charged meanings for aesthetic effect is the danger of objectifying the vulnerable and marginalised informal sector workers and their livelihoods. In India, this is more pronounced because of the entrenched, hierarchical social structure that offers little protection and almost no choice to subaltern communities labouring at these sites. Artists are then forced to ask themselves about the ethics of working on this subject, no matter how noble the intention, and their own privileged social locations that allow them to do so. This was a conversation Chaurasiya and I had from the beginning, and I suspect partly influenced his attempts to move away from an ethnographic approach that would only perpetuate an upper-caste/class gaze and reflect instead on the material qualities of waste.

In his large paintings, he combined traditional elements like watercolour and canson paper with matchstick heads, harking back to the format of earlier paintings but making them more layered. Though these are single works, they are haunted by the triptychs of dumps and landfills Chaurasiya composed as an art student.

It is in line with the notion of the "materiality paradox" that the economist Juliet Schor, author of *Plenitude: The New Economics of True Wealth*, has spoken about: "We are in an era... in which what people want from these goods is in large part their symbolic value, it has to do with their social meanings... when consumers are most hotly in pursuit of non-material meanings—when they care the most about the brand, the logo, what other people think etc., the brand value—they may be most prone to use up natural resources..."

This reality is what Chaurasiya's works try to capture, using the language of detritus to pose questions about the uncritical valorisation of immateriality, and showing how those utopian fantasies camouflage an inconvenient truth about the planetary effects of human occupation.

KHUSHBU PATEL
The Poetics of the Invisible

A lightning flash –
and, piercing the darkness,
the night heron's cry.
- Haiku by Matsuo Basho, trans. by Sam Hamill

A night secret.
A worm under the moon
bores in a chestnut.
- Haiku by Matsuo Basho, trans. by Jane Reichhold[6]

After much reflection, I settled on the haikus of seventeenth century Japanese poet Matsua Basho for Khushbu Patel's intense but deceptively lightweight works. Basho's exquisitely spare verse captures the experience of nocturnal vision. Patel's work is allusive like poetry, and almost too delicate to bear the weight of explanatory words. Her works might appear disconnected, but they are united by a dark humour, addressing death and an interest in playing with the visual regime of the artist. She wants to challenge the idea of physical perfection, investigate the metaphysics of the painterly surface and discern what inner beauty is (quite literally). It's an aesthetic of corners and crannies, cultivated in the gutter of her sketchbook—the sliver of shadow between the inner margins of two pages. It's an almost invisible strip in which dirt and grime accumulate. This is the home of her art, which she finds a way to replicate in architecture.

It is these unnoticed, oft-ignored spaces that she chooses to plant her art in, away from expectant eyes. It is this impulse that makes all works studies in imperceptible and unseen. I don't want to describe her individual works in minute detail, because they might break under my textual ministrations. Instead, I will present a series of categories that can offer a frame through which to look at her images. Patel trained as a painter and in these works, there is a desire to disturb habits of viewing and offer answers to questions that have always occupied painters—for example, what is depth? Or, how does an image mean something? Is art meant to draw the eye? Can it repel it? She turns her studio inside out, outside in. The veins on the floor give it the appearance of a living thing, the videos that result from medical imaging technology are tucked away in the building's orifices. The works have a life of their own, changing with each installation, depending on the site—animating the structure in which they are housed, hidden afflictions pulsating under the epidermis of the edifice, turning it into a gothic sensorium.

The delicate reticulate pattern beneath the viewers' feet and the placement of the little LCD screens out of their sight suggest an oblique engagement with death. It is the allegorical mode at work, the visible referring to the invisible, that which is outside the scopic regime. Death which is not knowable until it is upon us, defying the representability of the temporal world. At one level, the mode returns to the problem of mimesis—everything is a pale imitation of the unknowable, invisible real, so allusion rather than representation is a more authentic approach to confronting the extremities of life. Jisei or death poems are centuries old in the Japanese literary tradition, contending with the approach of death.

tradition. It is part of a larger practice of writing *jisei* ("death poems"), which continued for hundreds of years from as early as the seventh century by both monks and laypeople alike. Some of the earliest examples of jisei were appended to a will as a sort of farewell gesture to life. Gradually the jisei became a genre of its own, encompassing a range of poetic forms and moods. They are enigmatic, even ambivalent about death. It is because of this, perhaps, that the tradition is often overlooked.

Image above: Screenshot of an excerpt from Eugene Thacker, "Black Illumination: Zen and the poetry of death," *The Japan Times*, 2 July 2016.

The form of the haiku—17 syllables and three verse—was a popular one for the jisei. The exquisitely terse structure is dense but light, floating in the liminal strip between phenomenologies and somehow staying afloat. Basho's words seemed like the right accompaniment for Patel's understated approach that grapples with the discomfiting aspects of life; most importantly, as the ways in which it ends: disease, and eventually, death.

One afternoon, she and I sat in her studio discussing these connections between her work and Japanese aesthetics. As we flipped through her sketchbook, I showed her some haiku. She paused:

"MFA के time, मेरे एक प्रोफेसर ने वाबी-सबी के बारे में समझाया, मेरा काम भी कुछ वैसा ही है..."

Image above: Screenshot of a conversation with artist Khushbu Patel (Patel: "During my pursuit of a master's degree in fine arts, a professor explained the concept of 'wabi-sabi' to me, which is similar to my work").

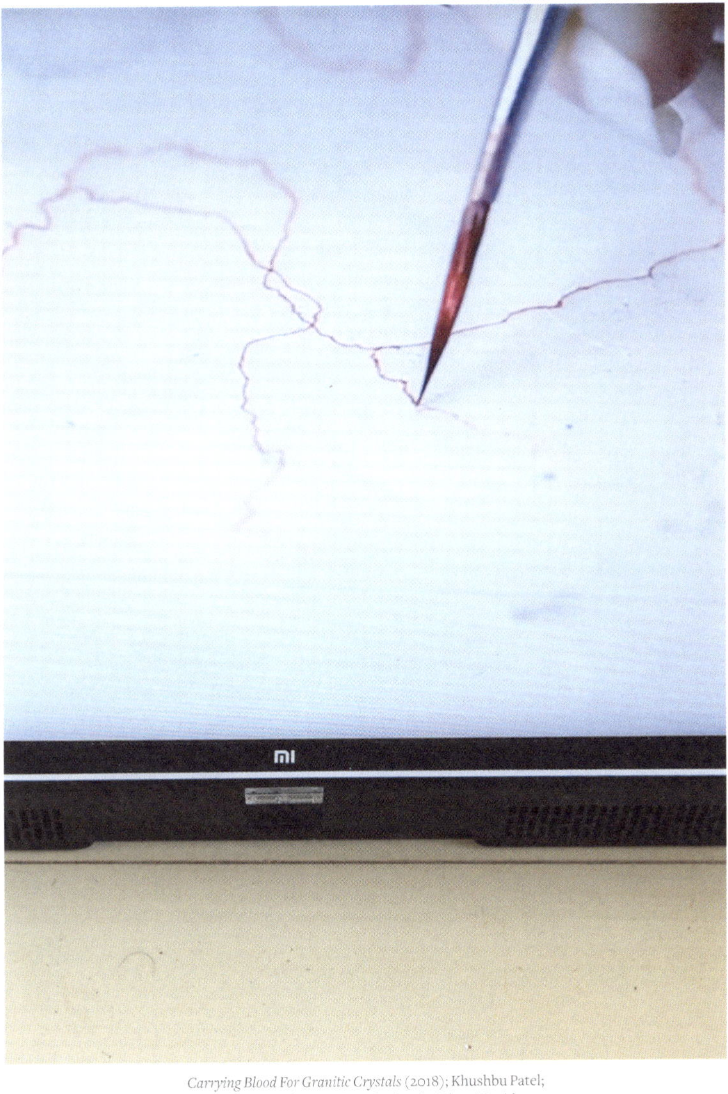

Carrying Blood For Granitic Crystals (2018); Khushbu Patel;
Video of project done at C340 during the Dharti Residency

Wabi-sabi is a Zen notion that lies in an appreciation of the imperfect, asymmetrical and incomplete, against the notion of "beautiful" that is based on harmony and wholeness. It is a perspective that values the unpretentious and attic; Basho's poems are also expressions of this idea.

An artist's originality is in the way she makes us stop in our tracks and look again at the familiar and worn. Patel's approach involves the manipulation of visual metaphors to make architectural space rhyme with the human body. For her, curating and production are simultaneous processes, as the mounting of the diagnostic imaging videos is integral to the questioning of spectatorial practices and a hierarchy that privileges outer beauty over reflecting inwards, a thought she cheekily renders by showing the internal workings of her own body.

Patel writes to me in July: "Here I have shared some of the links and quotations that I have referred to regarding my work. As Julia Kristeva asserts, in *Powers of Horror:*

A wound with blood and pus, or the sick, acrid smell of sweat, of decay does not signify death. In the presence of signified death—a flat encephalograph for instance—I would understand, react or accept. No, as in true theatre, without makeup or masks, refuse and corpses show me what I permanently thrust aside in order to live. These body fluids, this defilement, this shit are what life withstands, hardly and with difficulty, on the part of death. There I am the border of my condition as a living being."

Patel's work is haunted by the abject but doesn't confront it, retreating to the realm of the symbolic, not quite in the genre of Abject Art. It skirts the abject by touching upon the "sublime," that act of "naming" that is used to regulate the abject. That, Kristeva contends, lines the condition—"the abject is edged with the sublime... For the sublime has no object either."[7]

Rather than the confrontation with the pre-objectal that defines the abject, Patel's works epitomise what has been termed the "pathological sublime," a term coined by Mark Dery.

> pathological (and, by extension, teratological) body. A transport of aesthetic rapture that is equal parts horror and wonder, the Pathological Sublime is inspired by dark matter that holds beauty and repulsion in perfect, quivering tension. Refusing the moral gaze, the Pathological Sublime surrenders to the spell, at once aesthetic, psychological, and philosophical, of the fascinating (a word whose etymological roots are instructive: from the Latin fascinatus, "bewitch, enchant"), no matter the moral or ethical cost.

Image above: Screenshot of an excerpt from Mark Dery, "A Young Person's Guide to the Sublime," *Boingboing*, uploaded on 4 August, 2009.

It is this amoral, intense viewing that Patel's practice opens itself to. In many cultures, including the Abrahamic, the body is considered a signifier of the immoral and base, and aesthetic registers that address it—of which horror is an example—are devalued. This is certainly true of Western societies that have a Christian ethos. An attempt to induce physical sensation is regarded as less worthy of attention than that which appeals to the intellect or the "spirit"—worldly, temporal thrills being far inferior to the pleasures of the "soul" or "mind" or another incarnation of the non-body, depending on which period of Western history one is looking at. The "pathological sublime" is an opportunity to rethink this hierarchy, bringing into the domain of the awe -inspiring the workings of the human physique and anatomy.

When discussing her ideas for subjecting her skin to the dermatoscope or her otolaryngeal system to endoscopic examination or her vagina to an ultrasound scan, her use of her own body in creating works urges me to bring up the connection to performance art.

We talk about the Natyashastra's typology of bhavas or expressions—specifically the बीभत्स भाव/ *bibhatsa bhava*, that which pertains to disgust or the odious. As a classical Indian idea, it maintains a conceptual distance from the psychosexual notion of the abject while apprehending some of the same materials. The abject is, after all, "true theatre."

Can Patel's insertion of the medical images featuring the insides of her body into drains and slimy holes be considered a performance in the register of the *bhibatsa bhava*? Can we consider the medical imaging of one's own organs a performance of the invisible? Extreme bodily phenomena are moments when the abject becomes apparent, the materiality of the corpse being the ultimate manifestation of "death infecting life"—the transgression of boundaries, "what does not respect boundaries, positions, rules."[8] In Patel's work, what we see is the inner lining of the pathological sublime, the very film obscuring the abject—the surface that is the "sign of death," the flat encephalograph.

Michel Foucault posited "the medical gaze" as the practice of observation through which disease could be discerned, diagnosed and understood. He charts an anthropology of this gaze from the Enlightenment onwards and analyses this genre of looking as one that structures the modern history of Western medicine. Anatomo-clinical perception provides the axis along which the knowledge of the body and its pathology was developed.

"Death is disease made possible in life," writes Foucault,[9] pointing towards the liminality of the pathological sublime once again.

Patel's medical images can be situated in the art historical tradition of the memento mori—Latin for "remember you will die"—the medieval practice of thinking about mortality which spawned an entire visual genre. The only difference is that the nature of the sign has changed. Where skulls, clocks and dancing Grim Reapers were once were symbols of death, these electronic representations of human biology are iconic—resembling the invisible thing they refer to, "an image of death or the deterioration of the body that leads to it."[10]

The trajectory of the gaze is penetrative, beginning from the surface of the body to delve deeper and deeper into it, until the technology of the human eye is replaced by a non-human one. Lippit calls the X-ray image "with its simultaneous view of the inside and outside,"[11] an "impossible perspective."[12] The computerised strategies of today have been termed cyborg visuality.[13] Patel's list of medical imaging technologies:

- SKIN dermatologist used LED Dermascope.
- ENT examination:
  Ear testing called pneumatic otoscopy or tympanometry and it's also includes Audiometric testing.
  Nose testing called Nasal endoscopy- they pass a small telescope into the nostril to obtain a magnified view.
  Throat testing called Laryngoscope or endoscope.
- TVS Scan called Transvaginal Ultrasound Scan.
- SKIN BIOPSY examine in microscope.

Image above: A list of medical imaging technologies used by Patel.

The uncanny images of the interior organs were generated by radiological, sonographic, and LED technology, cryptic white and navy-blue blurs, the light from the screens causing them to resemble electronic glow-worms of some kind. As you recognise them to be snapshots from beyond what can be seen by the naked eye, you are made aware of your own mortality, your own body and its limits, once again escribing our selves onto the images.

In his essay "Eye and Mind," Merleau-Ponty talks about the way in which vision is determined by our bodies and the phenomenology of painting as an attempt to make what the artist sees in the world apparent to viewers. Merleau-Ponty describes the relationship between the body and the eye as co-constitutive, making physiology the axis of perception. He makes a case for the artist's body being the vehicle for him or her to use his or eyes and hands, seeing and rendering things in the world while being seen by the world.

According to him "all the problems of painting" are in this system of mutually made mobility and visuality, where the perceiver is perceived, and the world made available to his or her gaze.[14] The body isn't a passive entity, but one determining the contents of what and how objects are seen. The characteristics of the visual realm that are the painter's tools—colour, light, shape, depth—are all a result of the body's movement and are thus inseparable from it, which is why abstract, positive space is impossible.

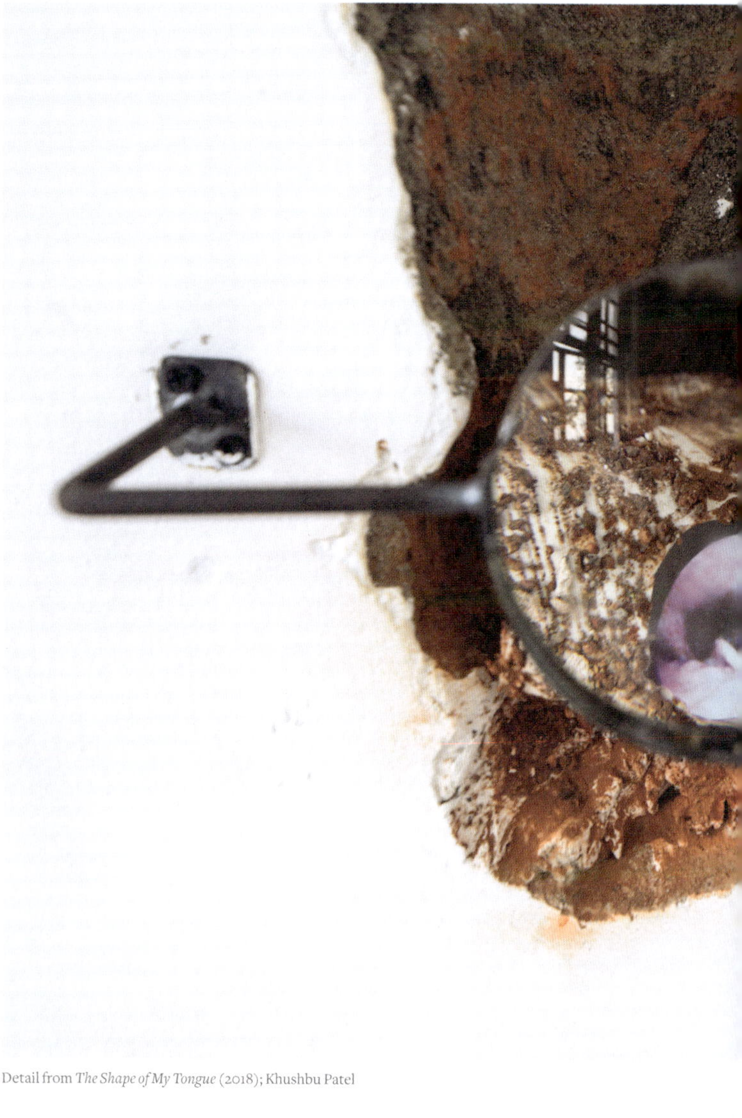

Detail from *The Shape of My Tongue* (2018); Khushbu Patel

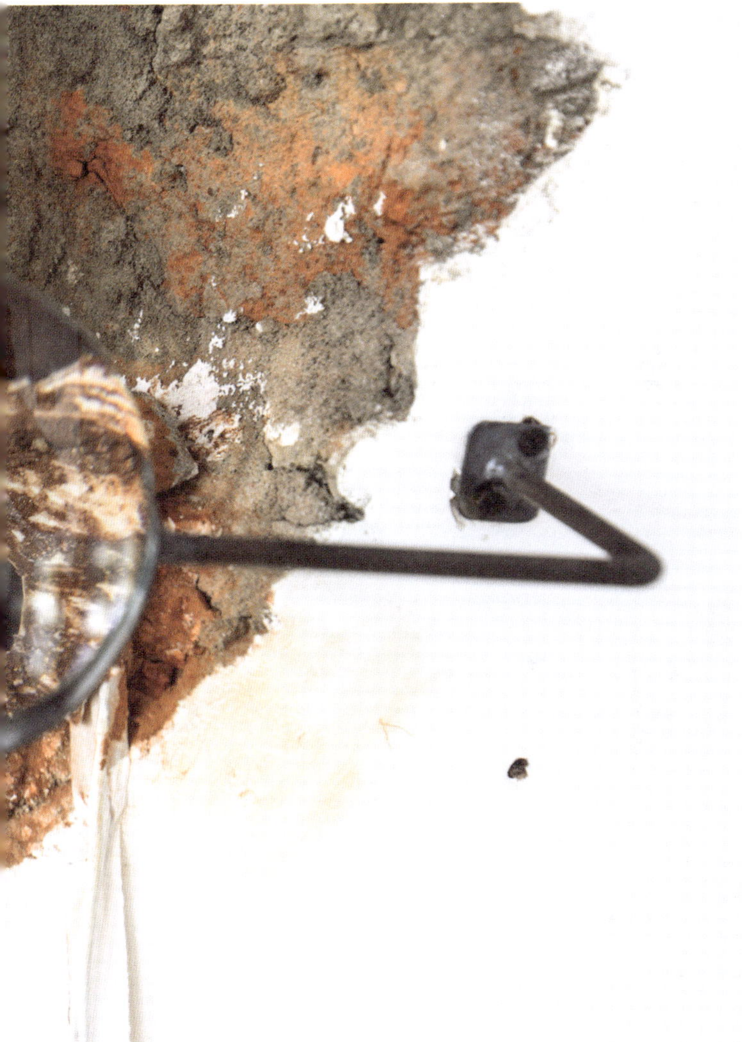

> What exactly does he ask of it? To unveil the means, which are nothing but visible, by which the mountain makes itself into a mountain before our eyes. Light, lighting, shadows, reflections, color, all these objects of his investigation are not altogether real beings; like ghosts, they have only visual existence. In fact they exist only at the threshold of profane vision; they are not commonly seen. The painter's gaze asks them how they make

Image above: Screenshot of an excerpt from Maurice Merleau-Ponty, "Eye and Mind," in *The Merleau-Ponty Reader*, eds. Ted Toadvine and Leonard Lawlor (Evanston: Northwestern University Press, 2007), 357.

At Dharti, Patel's painstaking application of slender painted lines onto the floor over the course of weeks had something of the artisanal labour of miniaturists about it. Viewers need a magnifying glass to even notice the work, implicating them and the artist in the act of looking: The artist, bent over, nose to ground moving her brush; the spectators peering closely, in all manner of attitudes, straining to follow the route she mapped.

As I hunch awkwardly and peep into the hole in the basement wall where Patel has planted her video of a cataract operation, I find my eye mirrored by the amorphous record of another eye. Was this not a performance too—the spectator's body rehearsing the artist's choreography? Indeed, as I climb up the stairs, careful not to touch the freshly painted red wrinkles on the floor, I find my own body becoming part of the work.

JAGRUT RAVAL
Roof of Silver: A Working Title

> "There is still some fire there," said Paracelsus, pointing toward the hearth. "If you cast this rose into the embers, you would believe that it has been consumed, and that its ashes are real. I tell you that the rose is eternal, and that only its appearances may change. At a word from me, you would see it again."
>
> "A word?" the disciple asked, puzzled. "The furnace is cold, and the re-torts are covered with dust. What is it you would do to bring it back again?"
>
> Paracelsus looked at him with sadness in his eyes.
>
> "The furnace is cold," he nodded, "and the retorts are covered with dust. On this leg of my long journey I use other instruments."
>
> "I dare not ask what they are," said the other

Image above: Screenshot of an excerpt from Jorge Luis Borges, "The Rose of Paracelsus," in *Collected Fictions*, trans. by Andrew Hurley (Penguin, 1999), 504-507.

Borges' tale of Paracelsus the alchemist complements Jagrut Raval's work for two reasons: firstly, it alludes to the actual medieval scholar ("Paracelsus") with that sobriquet, who wrote about bismuth in the sixteenth century. Secondly, it functions as an allegory for the relationship between art and those who seek to understand it, riffing off a very old relationship in intellectual history—that between reality and its truthful representation. Raval's practice builds on a meta-narrative last glimpsed in his *Philosopher's Wasps* (2017), continuing the exploits of a shadowy alter ego named Narad, an alchemist.

As an artist, Raval is concerned with the role of truth in narratives of the past and the future. In doing so, it is making claims about the epistemic possibilities of imagination—can art produce some sort of knowledge about the world by illuminating the space between what is perceptible and what is true? This is an exercise that becomes particularly valuable in a world of alternative facts, where shared pasts and common futures are being hijacked by dark forces.

The "furnace" and "retort" have been replaced by twenty-first century equipment, but the figure of the artist-as-alchemist returns in this series of works. The image of a visored Raval hunched over his induction stove, saucepan in hand, looms before me as I recall our conversations during the making of this work, resembling the mad scientist archetype.

Bismuth is an element with a relatively low melting point, which makes it ideal for experimenting with in one's basement—in this case, the one in C-340 Defence Colony, the site of the Dharti Art Residency. A mineral with a past, it was used by the Incas to make weapons and by German and Swiss artists of the Middle Ages to paint. Incidentally Paracelsus was Swiss too, which might explain a contemporaneous knowledge of bismuth. From a Tumblr page that Raval referenced during his research, he learned about a fifteenth century mineralogist called Georgius Agricola and found a possible title for his work:

He reported this in one of his earlier works: *Bermannus, sive de re metallica dialogus* (*Bermannus, or A Dialogue on Metallurgy*). Published in 1530, *Bermannus* presents a fictional conversation between the title character, a knowledgeable miner, and two scholars in other fields. The Hoovers included a passage from Bermannus in their translation of *De re metallica*, because it spells out Agricola's assertion that bismuth is a new metal:

Image above: Screenshot of an excerpt from the essay "Bismuth: The Sign of the Times" posted on the Tumblr account *Sodium Lamp*, URL: http://sodiumlamp.tumblr.com/post/117572889916/bismuth-sign-of-the-times.

The chemical qualities of bismuth make it a compelling substance for an artist to play around with. Apart from the iridescence of its oxidised surface, which causes it to shimmer like a kaleidoscope, once bismuth has melted it hardens into "hopper crystals":

- **Hopper crystals**

When a pool of molten bismuth solidifies it tends to form crystals like those in the first two pictures below. What seems to give these crystals their characteristic "hoppered" shapes is that there is more rapid growth at the edges of each face than at the center. (Spirals are probably associated with underlying screw dislocations.) Hoppering has not been much studied for scientific purposes, but has been noticed in many substances, including galena, rose quartz, gold, calcite, salt and ice.

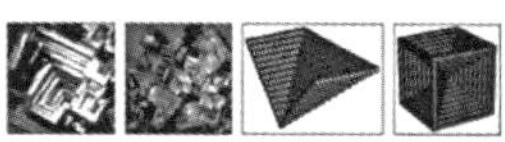

Image: Screenshot of an excerpt from Stephen Wolfram, "Chapter 8: Implications for Everyday Systems," *A New Kind of Science*, Online Webpage, URL: http://www.wolframscience.com/nks/notes-8-2—hopper-crystals.

Raval writes to me at the end of July: "I was drawn to its unique properties and fascinated by how it could very effortlessly create organic forms. On heating, it changes into something that looks in part futuristic, and in part astoundingly familiar—like ruins of an old civilisation." The inverted ziggurat-like crystals have an architectonic quality—glossy, solid and angular, almost as if intentionally designed. And yet, their strange lattice shapes and aleatory provenance resist attempts to read them simply as models or even sculptures.

The drawings and models of Lebbeus Woods, the American architect who was notorious for having only one actual building to his credit, were a major influence on Raval when he made this series. Woods' wild, retrofuturistic sketches were scaffolded by theory, riveting to behold and impossible to build, epitomising the mid-century conceptual architecture movement from whence he sprang, emphasis on "conceptual." Woods interrogated the abstract and manifest aspect of what architecture could do, pushing the boundaries of physics, geometry, urban planning and civil engineering.

Raval's work is infused with a similar gnomic quality, intensified by the mineral artefacts and technologies of moving image and sound. Speculation is at the heart of his practice, and the thrill of the counterfactual informs *Roof of Silver*, with its spooky evocations of outer space and otherworldly dystopias. The single-channel videos, a silver swathe of a floor punctuated by crystals and bismuth concretions on shelves are all suggestive of parallel universes and environments devoid of human presence, but somehow available to the human gaze.

"Projection—from the Latin projectionem (pro+jacere) meaning 'throwing forward, extension, projection'—indicates displacement, dislocation, transfer. At its core, geometry is a form modelled on

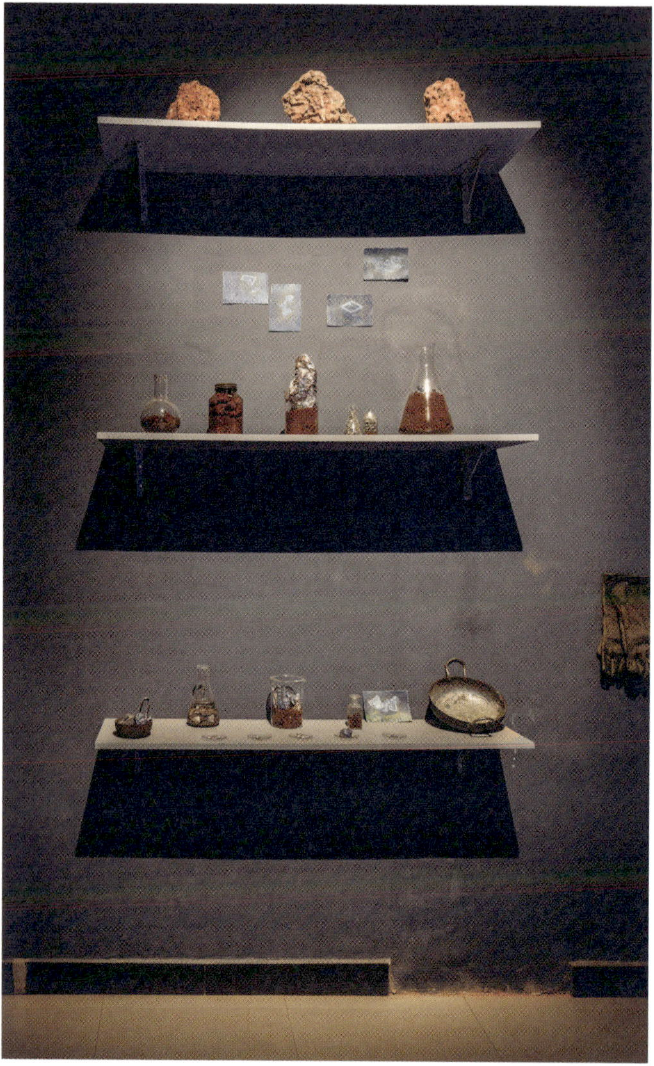

Notes from Emptiness (2018); Jagrut Raval

the properties of light rays... As such projective vision as a means of rationalising vision and space, underpinning perspectival rendering, cartography and architecture... & projected images elicit fantasy: they invite us to see things that are not there."[16]

The dark room or "black box" in which Raval' s works were mounted became a site of immersion, the carpet of light beneath my feet shifting colour like the crystals punctuating it. The surfaces in the videos hint at crusts of alien planets, dark contours of lands unmapped, and a non-human visual regime. I hesitate at the edge of the projection on the floor illuminating these quirky metallic structures, uncertain and endless scenes of an unfamiliar topography before me. I consider how to place myself in relation to them.

The philosophical discourse of speculative realism and Object Oriented Ontology, pervasive at the current moment, anchors the extra-terrestrial motifs of this series. Positioning his chemical experiments and digital video manipulations in a framework explicated by philosophers Timothy Morton and Graham Harman, Raval and I spent many hours over the course of the residency discussing metaphysics.

INT. C340 BASEMENT - DAY

JAGRUT: What is reality?
ME: Is what *humans* perceive the truth of the objects being perceived?
JAGRUT: If not, can humans know that truth about objects that exists outside their sensory capacities?

Image above: Screenshot of a conversation between Raval and the author.

In the history of ideas, these questions are ancient and have to do with the correspondence between things as they are and how humans can depict them. At one level, it's a yes/no question—with Plato inaugurating one tradition (no) and Aristotle another (yes) in Western philosophy. Since the Enlightenment, there has been an attempt to account for the world in terms of its relationship with human subjectivity. Immanuel Kant was the exponent of the notion of correlationism, a thought that became integral to the ideology of Romanticism, as concerned as it was with the individual's confrontation with the oft-mysterious natural world. The term refers to the correspondence or correlation between phenomena-in-themselves and phenomena-as-they-appear-to-humans. In his seminal work, *Hyperobjects*, Timothy Morton breaks it down: "The problem as correlationism sees is this: is the light on in the fridge when you close the door?"[17]

Morton uses the word "hyperobjects" to refer to "things that are massively distributed in space and time relative to humans."[18] He means anything from global warming to less lofty stuff, like Styrofoam. I'm feeling the horizontality of this prop. It's not this sense of being dwarfed by the infinite scale of the universe—no, that's the sort of "sublime" encounter that Romanticism privileged. In this room, these bits of bismuth seem to be sizing me up too. Like Caspar David Friedrich but with the mountains facing a distant dot of a human. Talk about being brought back to earth.

> a specific valence and definition that I elucidate in part 2. The overall aesthetic "feel" of the time of hyperobjects is a sense of *asymmetry* between the infinite powers of cognition and the infinite being of things. There occurs a crazy arms race between *what we know* and *what is*, in which the technology of what we know is turned against itself. The arms race sets new parameters for aesthetic experience

Image above: Screenshot of an excerpt from Timothy Morton, *Hyperobjects: Philosophy and Ecology After the End of the World* (Minneapolis: University of Minnesota Press, 2014), 16.

An aesthetic of asymmetry would not struggle to bring objects into the domain of human cognitive structures but play with the gap between objects as they are and objects as they appear. The Romantics asserted that imagination can become a kind of knowledge, and art is the only strategy to harness it. The scale and scope of hyperobjects require a new understanding of what imagination can yield through art.

Between the knowable and the unknown lies a whole plethora of aesthetic possibilities. Thinkers like Morton and Graham Harman represent a contemporary school of hardcore realism that affirms

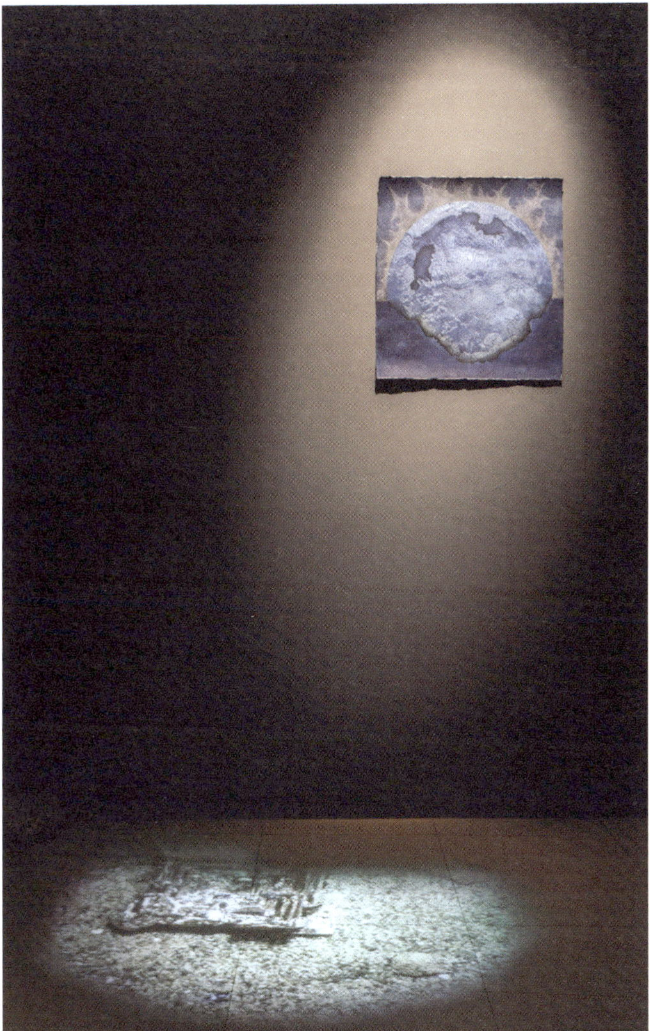

Notes from Emptiness (2018); Jagrut Raval

the "thing-ness" of objects as something ultimately beyond the grasp of humans, taking "real objects so seriously that it holds them to be irreplaceable by a conceptual model."[19] With a hyperobject like the Solar System or the Milky Way, what epistemic possibilities can art offer?

Can hyperobjects be captured in an art that departs from the values of Romanticism? Can they be glimpsed by "turning the technology of what we know against itself"?

Trawling through YouTube, Raval looked at a lot of footage from NASA's Curiosity Hazcam, revealing to human eyes for the first time what the Martian surface looked like.

One video's format mimicked that of actual NASA feed, another featured a reverse time-lapse close-up of the bismuth forms, a third used colour inversion to depict a territory incomprehensible in terms of human cognition. The opalescent bismuth crystals on the floor and rock-like lumps on shelves look like archaeological remains of an advanced civilisation, bringing to mind the Tungska event of 1908 when a meteorite crashed into Siberia.

The Surrealist preoccupation with the relationship between "figurative and verbal forms of representation"[20] was part of the universe of ideas Raval explored at Dharti. During the residency, his studio walls were adorned with pictures of Rene Magritte's works.

Magritte appeared to hold a view similar to OOO, playfully questioning correlationism in his own antic way: by challenging the link between "between things and their representation, and the interaction—often interference—between these ways of evoking an object."[21]

I'm reminded of Michel Foucault's eponymous essay on Magritte's *Ceci n'est pas une pipe* (1929) in which he invoked the concept of the calligram—a representation that combines text and image in a way such that they mutually emphasise each other's meanings. In terms of semiotics (the study of signs), a calligram can be thought of as a dance between two different orders of signs. Words are symbols, referring to things without looking like them, while pictures are icons: what you see is what you get. The calligram becomes an opportunity for both strategies of signification to come together in pursuit of the same referent. Foucault's reading of *Ceci n'est pas une pipe* is that it "unravels the calligram." It first establishes it—the hand that draws the pipe also writes the sentence, the shapes of both letters and picture rhyme with each other. Then it destabilises it by separating the picture and the text, so that the relationship between them is no longer constitutive but that of caption and image. In doing so, the "object itself escapes."[22]

Is it possible to appropriate the "unravelled calligram" as a conceptual category, to engage with works that try to capture hyperobjects? Perhaps, if we conceive of it as the space where two different schemes of representation—the symbolic and the iconic—unite and part, and in doing so access the interstice between the known and the ineffable. The bismuth crystals might be bits of interstellar debris; they are strewn on a floor like an allegory for parallel universes; the videos approximate the reality of other cosmic arrangements without committing to them. It is in this interplay of the steady comforts of scientific fact and the liberties of artistic interpretation, of the methods of experiment and exegesis, that the caligrammatic relationship between two schemes of reference becomes undone and divulges something.

The calligram is a phantom in *The Rose of Paracelsus*, the tension between referent and sign resolved by a sleight of hand and speech. The alchemist only reveals his magic to the reader once the narrator has left the story, the rose resurrected in his absence.

Notes

[1] Claire Bishop, "Installation Art," *Tate*, Issue 3, Spring 2005.

[2] Gil Perry, *Playing at Home: The House in Contemporary Art* (London: Reaktion Books, 2013), 15-19.

[3] Julio Cortazar, "Blow-up," *Blow-Up & Other Stories*, trans. by Paul Blackburn (New York: Collier Books, 1968), 111.

[4] Rosalind Krauss, "Video: The Aesthetics of Narcissism," October 1 (1976): 52.

[5] John Bellamy Foster, "Marx and the Rift in the Universal Metabolism of Nature," *Monthly Review: An Independent Socialist Magazine*, uploaded on 1 December, 2013. URL: https://monthlyreview.org/2013/12/01/marx-rift-universal-metabolism-nature/

[6] Gabor Terebess, "Matsuo Basho's haiku poems in romanized Japanese with English translations," *Terebess Asia Online*, URL: https://terebess.hu/english/haiku/matsuo.html

[7] Julia Kristeva, *Powers of Horror: An Essay on Abjection*, trans. by Leon S. Roudiez (New York: Columbia University Press, 1982), 11.

[8] Kristeva, *Powers of Horror: An Essay on Abjection*, 4.

[9] Michel Foucault, *The Birth of the Clinic: An Archaeology of Medical Perception*, trans. by A.M. Sheridan (Taylor & Francis e-library, 2003).

[10] Akira Mizuta Lippit, "Phenomenologies of the Surface: Radiation-Body-Image," *Qui Parle* 9, no. 2, 1996: 31–50.

[11] Lippit, "Phenomenologies of the Surface: Radiation-Body-Image," 34.

[12] Lippit, "Phenomenologies of the Surface: Radiation-Body-Image," 39.

[13] Amit Prasad, "Making Images/Making Bodies: Visibilizing and Disciplining Through Magnetic Resonance Imaging (MRI)," *Science, Technology, & Human Values* 30, Issue 2, 2005: 292.

[14] Maurice Merleau-Ponty, "Eye and Mind," in *The Merleau-Ponty Reader*, eds. Ted Toadvine and Leonard Lawlor (Evanston: Northwestern University Press, 2007), 355.

[15] Robert E. Krebs, *The History and Use of Our Earth's Chemical Elements: A Reference Guide* (Westport: Greenwood Press, 2006), 221.

[16] Liz Kotz, "Video Projection: The Space Between Screens," in *Art and the Moving Image: A Critical Reader*, ed. Tanya Leighton (London: Tate Publishing, 2008), 371-372.

[17] Timothy Morton, *Hyperobjects: Philosophy and Ecology after the End of the World* (Minneapolis: University of Minnesota Press, 2014), 7.

[18] Morton, *Hyperobjects: Philosophy and Ecology After the End of the World*, 1.

[19] Graham Harman, "The Road to Objects," *continent*. 3, No. 1 (2011): 179.

[20] Hal Foster, Rosalind Krauss, Yves-Alain Bois and Benjamin H.D. Buchloch, *Art Since 1900: Modernism, Antimodernism, Postmodernism*, (London: Thames & Hudson, 2004), 18.

[21] Hal Foster et al., *Art Since 1900: Modernism, Antimodernism, Postmodernism*, 212.

[22] Michel Foucault, "Ceci n'est pas une pipe," trans. by Richard Howard, *October* 1 (Spring, 1976): 12.

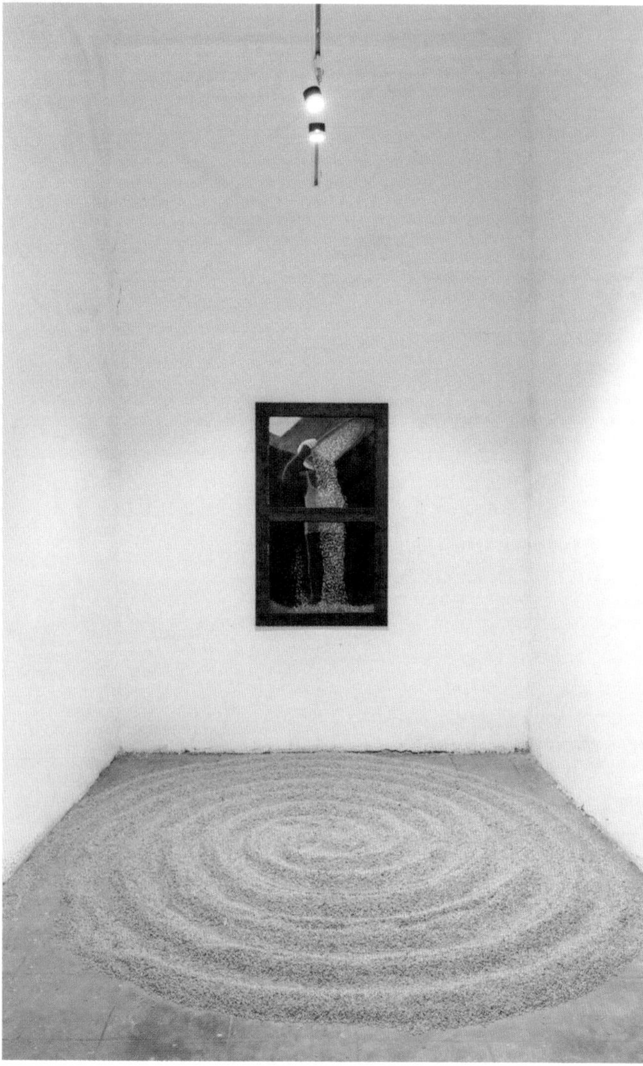

The Harvest (2018); Sonia Rodrigues Sabharwal;
Mixed media; 30" x 50"

Panjim 175

Curated by Vivek Menezes and Swati Salgaocar

Venue PWD Complex

Curatorial Note

PANJIM 175

Participants *Waylon D'Souza, Kausalya Gadekar, Parvesh Java, Harshada Kerkar, Neha Kudchadkar, Chaitali Morajkar, Sonatina Mendes, Sandesh Naik, Shilpa Mayenkar Naik, Loretti Pinto, Sonia Rodrigues Sabharwal, Nishant Saldanha, Pritha Sardessai, Rajeshree Thakker, Bookworm Trust, Liz Kemp, Rhea D'Souza, Goa Heritage Action Group, Goa Bird Conservation Network and Carl D'Silva*
Special Project Curators *Vivek Menezes & Swati Salgaocar*
Curatorial Assistant *Daphne de Souza*
Project Supported by

vimson
Shivanand Salgaocar Group

Precisely 175 years ago, the tiny riverside city of Panjim ascended to "urbs prima" in the Estado da Índia, which once extended from the Konkan coastline to Mozambique in East Africa, and Macau and Timor at the other extreme of the Indian Ocean. This unexpected rise signalled something entirely new in the world: native dominance within the colonial context. Panjim was the first planned city in India, that was built by locals for their own purposes even while the Portuguese still maintained nominal control. This is one reason Goa's capital feels—and is!—so comprehensively different from other cities in India, most especially those built by the British during their Raj. Throughout its history, this deceptively quiet city has functioned as an assertive civilisational statement by Goans of all religious and economic backgrounds, who constantly strived to seize meaningful advantages when they appeared during Portuguese proto-democratic and republican episodes throughout the 19th and 20th centuries.

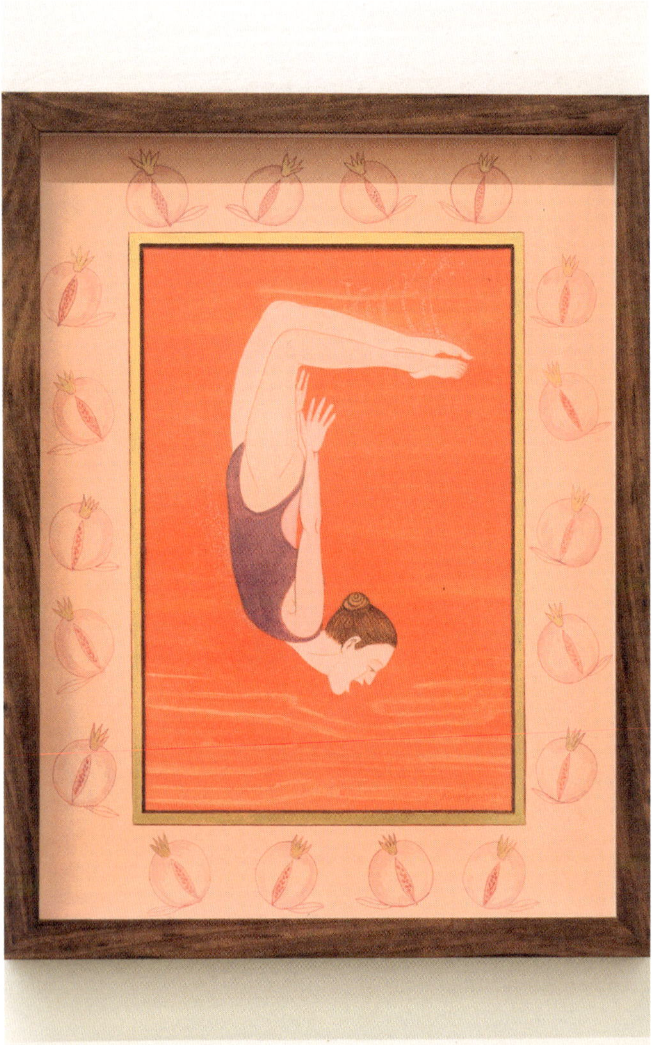

The Sacred Synchrony 1-12 (2018); Kausalya Gadekar;
Gouache on paper; 11.5" x 15"

Panjim 175

VIVEK MENEZES

Even by the multidisciplinary standards of Serendipity Arts Festival 2018, the challenges and opportunities bound up in the "Panjim 175" exhibition stood apart in complicated ways that demanded multidimensional curatorial approaches. It was the main exhibition of Goa-based artists for an event that sought to cement its value for India's smallest state. At the same time, it was poised to address the vacuum created by state apathy regarding the hugely significant historical anniversary of the moment Panjim was catapulted to global significance, as the capital of the transnational Estado da India Portuguesa. There were two other civic motivations: to demonstrate what a carefully programmed, beautifully conceived arts center could bring to the riverfront city by providing alternate views and ideas to the destructive and wasteful changes being wrought in the name of smart city development. But, primarily, Swati Salgaocar and I wanted to introduce people to the city we live in and love, with its immense potential for the future, and an astounding, luminous past that has profoundly influenced modern India.

Taking a break from the raging cholera outbreak in Sindh in 1847, the 26-year-old lieutenant, remarkable scholar, polyglot and thoroughbred scoundrel Richard Francis Burton sailed from Bombay to the newly named "Nova Goa" at the mouth of Mandovi river. Just three years earlier, the tiny city had become the capital of the vast *Estado da India* maritime empire of the Portuguese: nerve centre of an extensive network sprawling from Mozambique in East Africa all the way across to Timor at the farthest end of the Lesser Sunda Islands very close to Australia. Published in 1851, the bilious, screamingly funny *Goa and the Blue Mountains* was this Victorian writer's very first book, and—if you peer carefully between the sheets piled with generous heapings of hostility—it remains an essential documentation of the material, social and cultural divergences between British and Portuguese colonialism in India.

The excursion started off rather agreeably. On his first morning, Burton awakens very happily on his *pattimar*: "The air was soft and fragrant, at the same time sufficiently cool to be comfortable. A thin mist rested upon the lower grounds and hovered half way up the hills, leaving their palm-clad summits clear to catch the silvery light of dawn. Most beautiful was the hazy tone of colour all around contrasted with the painfully vivid tints and the sharp outlines of an Indian view seen a few hours after sunrise."[1] But then he recounts, "horror of horrors" as his mood deteriorates rapidly and permanently, when a blithe young Goan man comes aboard, first surprising Burton by addressing him in English, then liberally helping himself to sherry, eating "at least a dozen plantains" before "trying on our hat... defiling our brushes and combs with his limp locks, redolent of rancid cocoa-nut oil and glancing with fearful meaning at our tooth-brushes"[2]

All this is inconceivable to the Raj-era racist, whose account rather predictably erupts throughout with splenetic fits of outrage about the collective Goan refusal to understand proper subservience. Burton writes with great ire: "the black Indo-Portuguese is an utter radical; he has gained much by Constitution, the 'dwarfish demon,'" which sets everybody by the ears at Goa. Hence it is he who will take the first opportunity in a conversation with a foreigner to extol Lusitanian liberty to the skies, abuse English tyranny over, and insolence to, their unhappy Indian subjects and descant delightedly upon the probability of an immediate crash in our Eastern empire. And, as might be expected, although poverty sends forth thousands of black Portuguese to earn money in foreign lands, they prefer the smallest competence at home, where equality allows them to indulge in a favourite independence of manner utterly at variance with our Anglo-Indian notions concerning the proper demeanour of a native towards a European."[3]

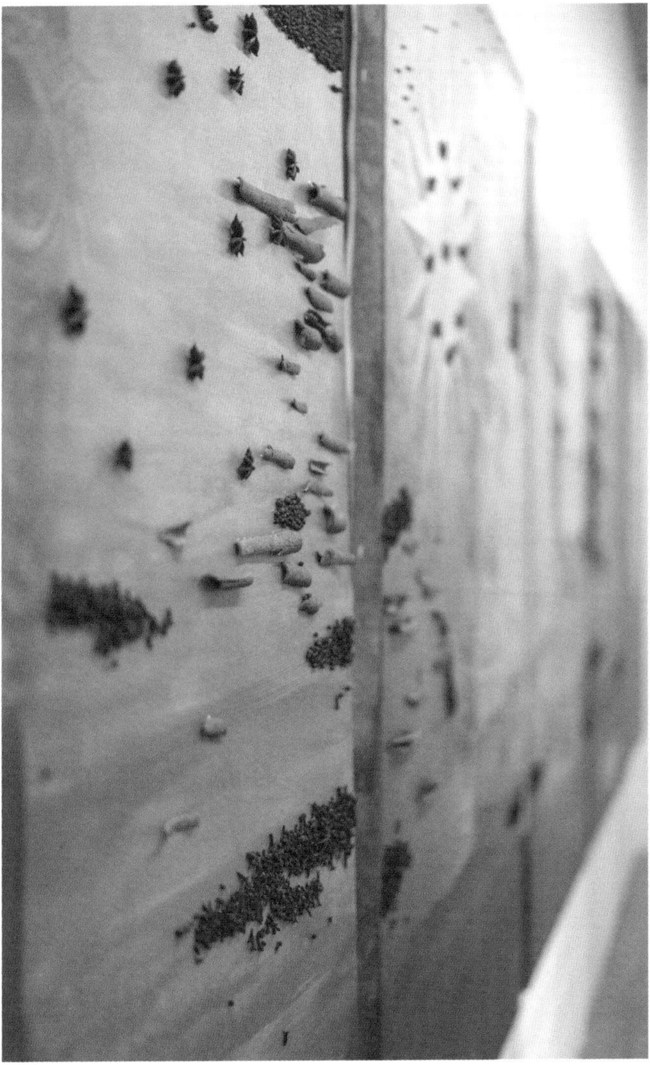

Detail from *Nova Goa—Trade Center of the World* (2018); Sandesh Naik;
Acrylic on canvas and mixed media; 20' x 6'

Burton is referring to Portugal's decidedly liberal thrust, which was first triggered from the famous "Pombaline Reforms" initiated by Sebastião José de Carvalho e Melo, the Marquis de Pombal, who was de facto head of state in Portugal from 1750-77. During this time, he expelled the Jesuits—who had become politically and economically dominant in Goa—while fostering secular education, streamlining administration, abolishing slavery along with lesser genealogical discriminations and greatly expanding both writ and idea of equal citizenship for "all Portuguese" whether in Europe, or Goa and Brazil. By 1822, the Goans were already electing their own rebellious representatives to parliament in Lisbon, and after some back-and-forth in this early democratic experiment, Bernardo Peres da Silva became the first native to be appointed Governor of the *Estado* in 1835. This episode was itself aborted after 17 days by vehement resistance, and an eventual coup by the "white" and mestiço (mixed race) lobbies.

Nonetheless, when Burton sailed up to the new colonial capital, an astonishing and unprecedented rout was well underway, as the balance of power shifted definitively from European hands to Indian, even within the contours of the colonial state. While the Portuguese did hold on (as they eventually did for another 114 years, well after the British themselves were compelled to hand over the famous freedom at midnight), they managed that feat only under severe duress, via an unending series of painful concessions and compromises with increasingly assertive native elites. This unavoidable reality underlies the brash young imperialist's wounded ego, and palpable anguish about the inverted social order he perceived all around him. As the American historian Dane Kennedy writes in the Introduction to the excellent University of California edition of *Goa and the Blue Mountains*, Burton "attributes the decline of Portuguese power in India to the misguided policy of dismantling the racial and religious boundaries between ruler and ruled... [with] direct relevance for the policies the British pursued."[4]

But politics isn't everything, and it certainly wasn't to Burton, whose irrepressibly heightened sense of aesthetics eventually overwhelmed his many discomfitures. "An entertainment at the house of a Goanese noble presents a curious contrast to the semi-barbarous magnificence of our Anglo-Indian 'doings,'" he remarks, increasingly less grudgingly, "in the one [meaning British India] as much money as possible is lavished in the worst way imaginable; the other [of the Goans] makes all the display which taste, economy and regard for effect combined produce. The balls... are probably the prettiest sights of the kind in Western India. There is a variety of costumes, which if not individually admirable, make up an effective *tout de ensemble*; even the dark faces, in uniforms and ball dresses, tend to variegate and diversify the scene."[5]

Burton allows, "The bands are better than the generality of our military musicians, European as well as Native, and the dancing, such as it is, much more spirited...The dinner parties resemble the other entertainments in economy and taste; the table is decorated, as in Italy, with handsome China vases...the cooking is all in the modified French style common to the South of Europe."[6] And that unusually knowing degree of eclectic cosmopolitanism isn't only restricted to the table, "we saw an unmistakable Lakshmi borne in procession amongst Christian images... and on the other hand, many a Gentoo [meaning non-Christian] has worn a crucifix for years, with firm faith in the religious efficacy of the act." The preponderance of accumulated evidence leads to Burton's rather glum conclusion about Goan society, that "there is perfect equality, political as well as social, between the two colours."[7]

This singular prevalence of parity in Portuguese India in 1847 can be usefully contrasted with Winston Churchill's sentiments and comments about British subjects in the rest of the subcontinent, made almost exactly 100 years later, which are perfectly summed up in his admission to Leo Amery, the Secretary of State for India, "I hate Indians. They are a beastly people with a beastly religion."[8] Almost exactly the same time, while purposefully engineering the unconscionable Bengal Famine of 1943 (where up to two million died) he argued "the starvation of anyway underfed Bengalis is less

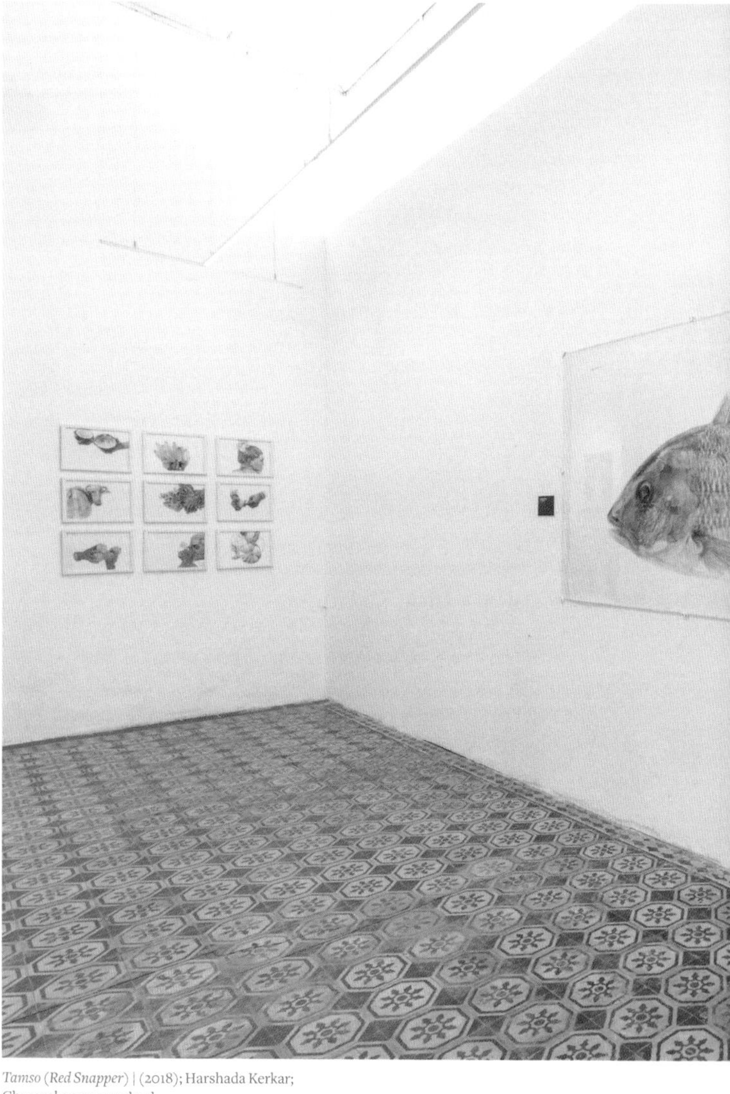

Tamso (*Red Snapper*) | (2018); Harshada Kerkar;
Charcoal on paper; 5' x 4'

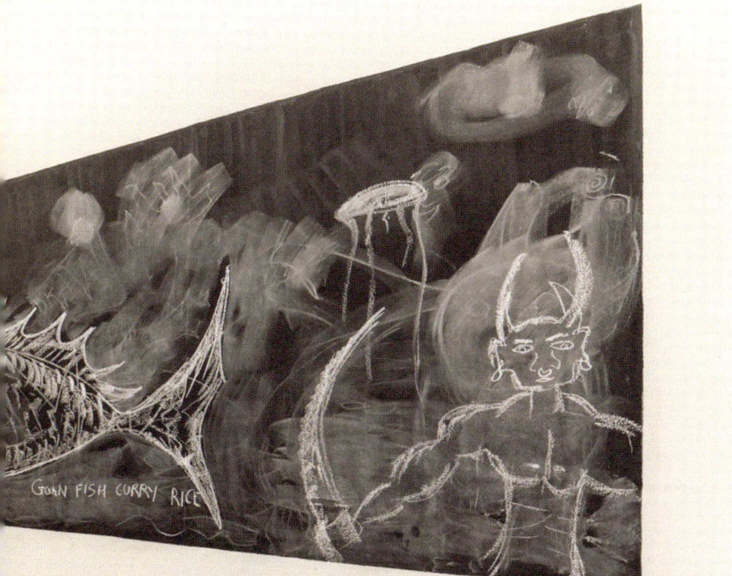
GOAN FISH CURRY RICE

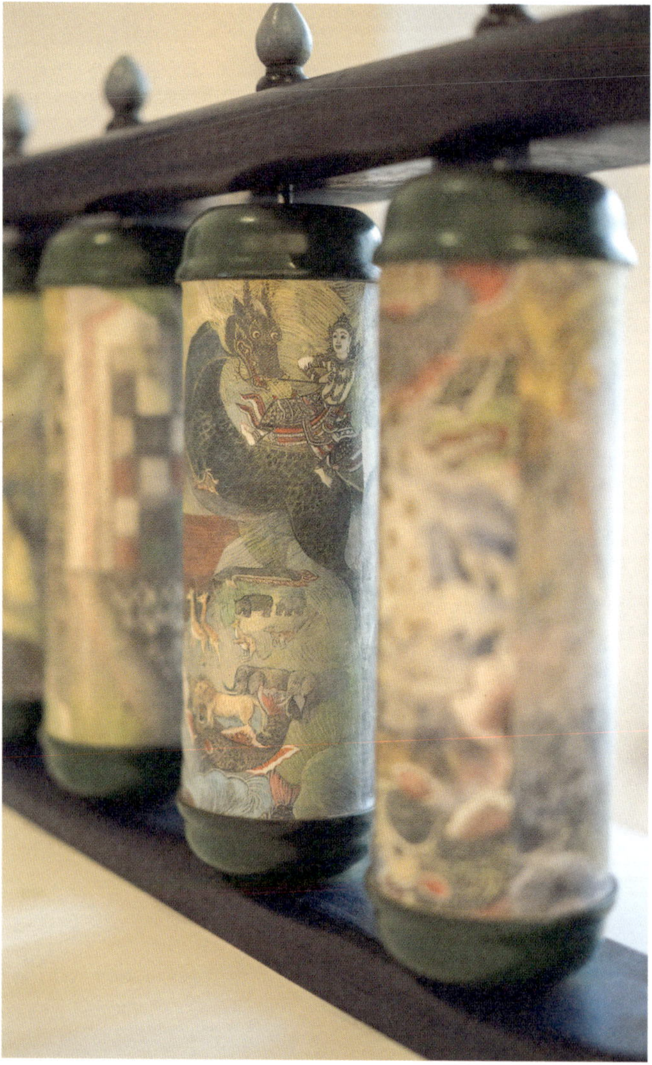

Prayer Wheels for Goa (2018); Rajashree Thakkar;
Mixed media; 27" x 13"

serious" compared to "sturdy Greeks" to whom he was diverting grain surpluses. This most odious veteran of the Raj chose to blame the Indian victims for the famine which killed them, for the offense of "breeding like rabbits" and when informed of excruciating suffering, callously responded, "why hasn't Gandhi died yet?"[9]

Of course by then, Churchill was already nearly 70 years old, and at the very end of his political usefulness. All puffed up with victory in World War II, he had declared, "I have not become the King's First Minister in order to preside over the liquidation of the British Empire" but that's precisely what happened in bewilderingly short order. Now the tables turned, and it was Jawaharlal Nehru's turn for timeless rhetoric, as exemplified by his stirring address to the Constituent Assembly on the 15th of August, 1947, "Long years ago, we made a tryst with destiny; and now the time comes when we shall redeem our pledge, not wholly or in full measure, but very substantially. At the stroke of the midnight hour, when the world sleeps, India will awake to life and freedom. A moment comes, which comes but rarely in history, when we step out from the old to the new—when an age ends, and when the soul of a nation, long suppressed, finds utterance."[10]

It should come as no surprise that this new voice was substantially seeded by the only natives of the subcontinent who had already experienced expansive freedoms for several generations, precisely Burtons uppity "black Portuguese." The first Indian editor of the Times of India was Frank Moraes, originally of Santa Cruz village near Panjim. The first Secretary of the Indian National Congress was Justice Kashinath Telang (he was also the first Indian Vice-Chancellor of Bombay University), whose roots are in Pernem. There are countless other names in this list of national pioneers, including the Goans whose fingerprints can be found all over the two great unifying forces of modern India—Saligao's Anthony de Mello founded the Board of Cricket Control of India, and also chaired the committee which created the Asian Games, while the irresistible "Sound of Bollywood" was originally created by a host of Goan musicians, ranging from Majorda's Anthony Gonsalves to Ponda's singing sisters, Lata Mangeshkar and Asha Bhonsle.

Although this particular aspect of cultural history is barely acknowledged, and even less understood, it's much the same for Indian art. Just a decade after Richard Burton swashbuckled his way around Goa, the Sir Jamsetjee Jeejeebhoy School of Art was founded in 1857, and from its inception disproportionately burgeoned with students from Portuguese India. Within a couple of decades, its Director was proudly boasting about the facility of his "Goanese" favourites who were regularly winning prizes at the Bombay Art Society's exhibitions. Most prominent amongst these was Antonio Xavier Trindade from Sanguem, who moved swiftly from tinting photographs for Raja Deen Dayal, to become his alma mater's first Indian star faculty member, and the first Indian Superintendent of the influential Reay Workshops which focused on producing "beautiful and useful objects."

In 1920, Trindade excelled himself by winning the Gold Medal of the Bombay Art Society, for his stunning allegorical masterpiece *Flora* (which is on everyday display in Panjim, at the Indian headquarters of Lisbon-based Fundação Oriente). It's an amazing painting, in part because of its superbly skillful technique in oils, but especially for its subject matter. Pictured as the Roman fertility goddess is Florentina Trindade, the artist's wife, who was already mother to his eight children, posed and clothed most unlike what you might expect from an Indian woman painted by her husband in that era. Considering that Rabindranath Tagore only formally started his university at Shantiniketan the following year, you might guess that Trindade's breakthrough would be acknowledged as the foundation stone of Indian modernism. But you would be wrong.

This glaring lacuna persists because, like so many other aspects of Indian scholarship about culture, the Establishment-generated history of Indian modernism is riddled with biases and misconceptions. As the "Young Turk" of pre-Independence Indian art, P. T Reddy wrote, "there used to be a healthy feud between Bombay and Calcutta Art Schools. Each school was rejecting the other as 'western' and at the same time proclaiming itself Indian. Actually both followed the European as well as Indian traditions and techniques."[11] But after 1947, the Goa-Bombay narrative—with its cohort of Muslim, Parsi and Goan exemplars from mostly working class backgrounds—was erased from art history, in favour of the upper-caste Hindu circle of the Tagores and the Bengal School. It took until the twenty-first century, with its market-driven reassessment of Indian art of global significance, for some kind of balance to be restored.

From today's perspective, Goa's contributions to the billion-dollar art market seem obvious, and everyone agrees that Panjim is the perfect location to host ambitious cultural events of both national and international significance. But none of that was anywhere on the horizon until 2007, when the aptly named exhibition *Aparanta: The Confluence of Contemporary Art in Goa*, for which I served among the organisers, was presented. The exhibition was curated by Ranjit Hoskote in the magnificent heritage headquarters of the Goa Medical College—the first such institution in Asia—which had been irresponsibly tendered out by the state government to a Delhi company that submitted plans to convert the building into a mall. Here, for the first time ever, explicit links were made between the youngest generation of artists working in Goa and their world-renowned predecessors, like Francis Newton Souza (of Saligao), Vasudeo Gaitonde (of Uccasaim) and Laxman Pai (of Margao) who had all been integral to the Progressive Artists Movement of 1940s Bombay, as well as to non-native artists whose work is profoundly affected by meaningful connections to Goa, such as Dayanita Singh and Baiju Parthan.

At that time, Hoskote wrote in the curatorial essay, "Goan art has long been an invisible river, one that has fed into the wider flow of Indian art but has not always been recognised as so doing. This, despite the presence of such master spirits of Goan origin—active throughout the colonial, postcolonial and globalisation periods... The glossy

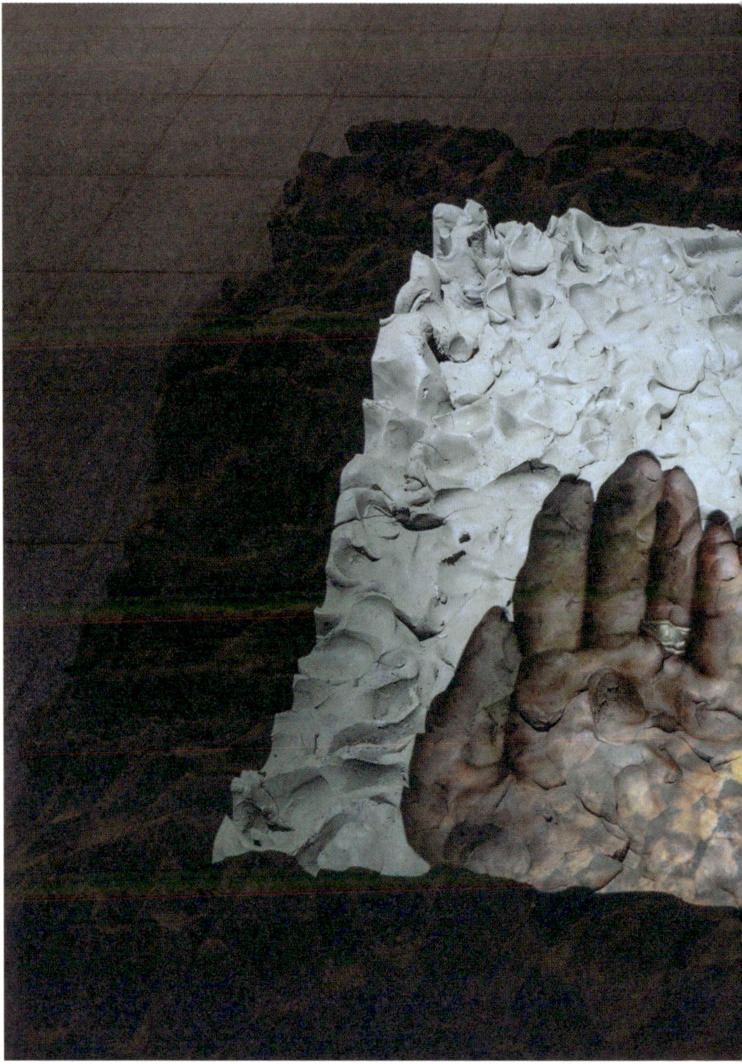

Inheritance (2018); Neha Kudchadkar;
Film Projection on unfired clay, Stoneware, Mixed media; Variable dimensions

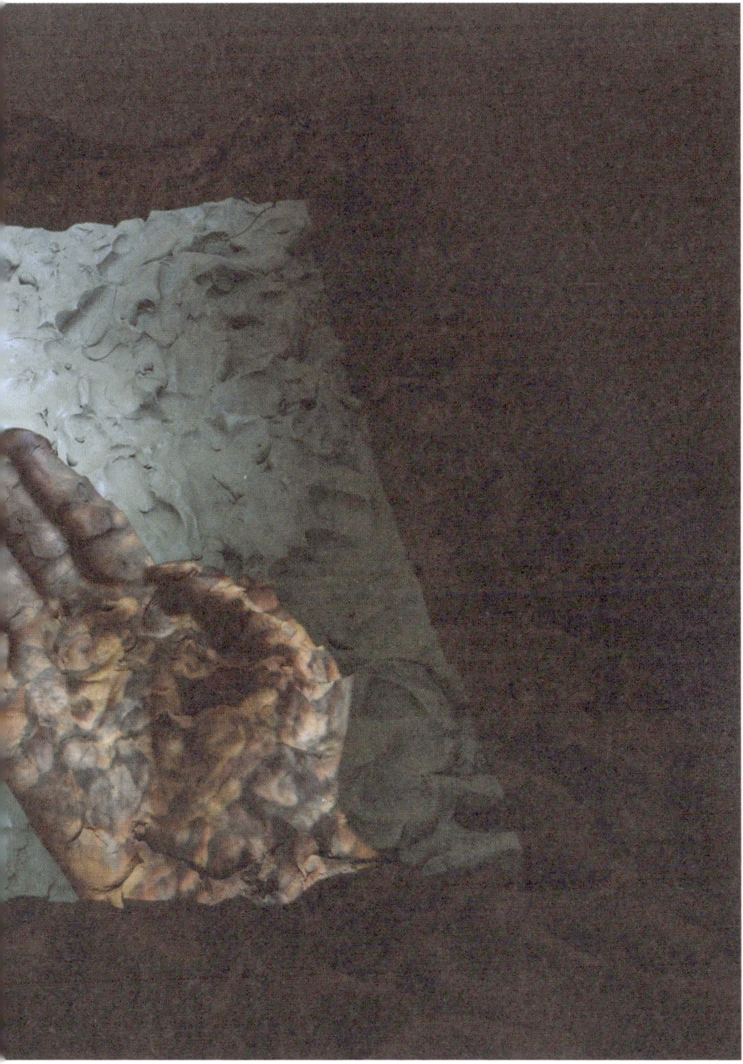

stereotype is a more effective blinder than the heated needle of the mediaeval executioner: the associations of sun, sand, sex and carnival with Goa are so pervasive that even the better informed denizens of the Indian art world seem unaware of the vibrancy of the art scene in Goa [which] finds its definition around a number of inspired individuals who defy the apathy of India and the defeatism of their peers; around groups of artists acting collegially towards a higher common purpose; and around the cluster of compelling psychic and historical contents that spur them on to artistic exploration."[12]

With remarkable insight, Hoskote described the prevailing problems: "Goa has brilliant, meteorically brilliant artists. But the lack of a context has left them afloat in a void of discussion. Geographical contiguity does not mean that Goa and mainland India share the same universe of meaning: Goa's special historic evolution, with its Lusitanian route to the Enlightenment and print modernity, its Iberian emphasis on a vibrant public sphere, its pride in its ancient internationalism avant la lettre, sets it at a tangent to the self-image of an India that has been formed with the experience of British colonialism as its basis. The relationship between Goa's artists and mainland India has, not surprisingly, been ambiguous and erratic, even unstable." And then the curator took a firm stand: "*Aparanta* is intended to make a major statement: that Goa, far from being a cultural backwater remote from the centres of Mumbai, Delhi and Bangalore, is a seed-bed of artistic excellence."[13]

Fast forward just over a decade, and exactly like Nehru's marvellous contentions about the country in 1947, it is readily apparent the *Aparanta* gambit succeeded "not wholly or in full measure, but very substantially." Within days of exhibition opening, the crowds who attended had spearheaded renewed attention for the gorgeous built landscape of Panjim, kicking off highly effective civil society protests against the venue being handed over for ill-conceived "development." It was saved for the public, and today, along with the renovated eighteenth-century Maquinez Palace next door, serves as the venue for the International Film Festival of India each November. This huge, global event kicked off an extraordinary cultural "high season" in Panjim that no one could have predicted in 2007—in the first week of December is the unique Goa Arts + Literature Festival, of which I am a co-founder and co-curator, along with the eminent Konkani writer Damodar Mauzo, followed by the Serendipity Arts Festival (SAF), with its own dramatic reinvention and adaptive reuse of the heritage venues along the Mandovi riverfront. From its inception in 2016, this festival's efforts have comprehensively shaken up our idea of what is possible, with its game-changing ambition and world-class execution, and constant emphasis on experimentation.

Precisely this backdrop compelled and motivated the multi-faceted *Panjim 175* (2018) at the third edition of SAF, which coincided with the 175th anniversary of its ascension to the capital of the *Estado da India*. Similar to what its direct antecedent *Aparanta* tackled over a decade earlier, it was self-consciously conceived to be more than simply another art exhibition, but extending to elements of manifesto, declaration of intent and expressing an alternate idea of India itself. The exhibition's many-layered character derived from the desire to address convergent compulsions: an honest representation of the wealth of artists working in Goa, and the showcasing of Panjim's cultural heritage and ecological significance, as well as the necessity to provide counterpoints to the wasteful contemporary interventions rampantly brutalising the city, with the worst excesses being committed under the Orwellian misnomer of "smart city."

Swati Salgaocar and I laid out several of these separate goals in the curatorial note. We wrote, "Throughout its history, the deceptively quiet city has functioned as an assertive civilisational statement by Goans of all religious and economic backgrounds. Here, citizens of Goa acquired and experienced equal civil rights, several generations before other Indians could manage the same. They self-confidently developed numerous important institutions, many decades ahead of other cities of Asia: the first public library, the first comprehensive school for girls, the first modern municipal council. Much the same occurred within the cultural ambit, as the art and artists of Goa substantially seeded the development of contemporary and modern Indian art, most prominently via a series of exemplars: Trindade, Fonseca, Souza, Gaitonde, Laxman Pai."

While many of those names have become recognised by the art market, we argued "much less known, and quite often purposefully misunderstood, are their extraordinary successors in the twenty-first century. For an eye-opening change, you will see several of these represented in *Panjim 175* at Serendipity Arts Festival 2018, located in the old state Public Works Department complex at the foot of the old and new Patto bridges in Sao Tome. More than any other urban entity in India, Panjim embodies ideas of community across the sectarian lines that usually divide the subcontinent. That remarkable legacy is crucial to [our exhibition], which brims with the enthusiastic support and participation of *bhaille ani bhitorle*, outsiders and insiders of every possible background. Together, and on their behalf, the curatorial team welcomes one and all to this labour of much love and intense collaboration."

With this bare outline, Swati and I—who were joined in our efforts by the excellent Daphne de Souza—tackled numerous issues and goals that do not generally go along with art exhibitions. We wanted to showcase our crumbling, but rather lovely riverside venue as an example of how user-friendly arts and culture venues can be created almost anywhere on the Panjim waterfront. To accomplish this, and keep people at our venue long enough to get this central point, we dedicated two prominent spaces for an extensive "museum shop" selling clothing, books, and various memorabilia connected to *Panjim 175* and an excellent café featuring filter coffee, baked goods and a small tapas menu from the beloved city institution, Black Sheep Bistro.

Because it was apparent that the city's momentous 175th anniversary was going unrecognised, with no attention paid by either the local or state government, we decided to combat the apathy, by commissioning two exclusive posters for display all over the city, and, organising free distribution of high-quality poster prints at the venue.

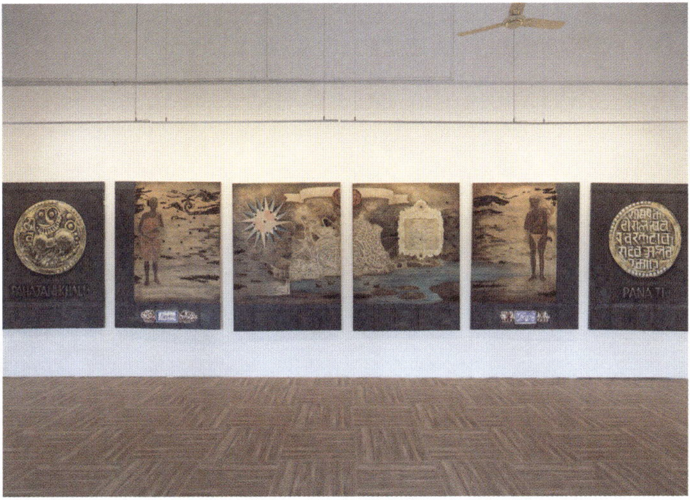

Nova Goa—Trade Center of the World (2018); Sandesh Naik;
Acrylic on canvas and mixed media; 20' x 6'

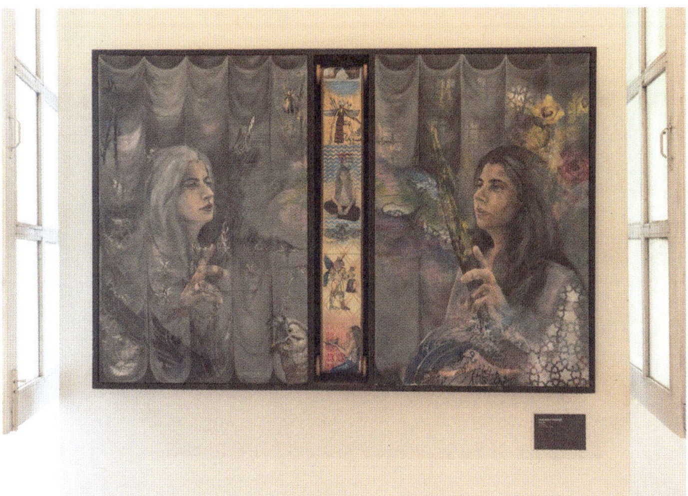

Descent (2018); Rajashree Thakkar;
Mixed media; 57" x 37" x 3"

As the symbol of *Panjim 175*, we chose the century-old mermaid, who reigns centrepiece of her eponymous garden on the waterfront. It seemed perfectly suited in its ambiguous relevance to the fluid Goan identity. Does it belong on sea or land? Does it belong to any standard categories of classification? Is it European or Indian? Shilpa Mayenkar Naik—who had made her spectacular exhibition debut at *Aparanta*, rendered her version faithfully minute to the original, but in the style of *azulejos*, the emblematic Islamic-Iberian ceramic tradition that can be seen in several places in Goa. Equally unforgettable, the California-educated animator and film-maker Nishant Saldanha pictured the same subject surrounded by carefully rendered native flowers. Both images became rapidly popular: first on social media and then through the thousands of copies that were picked up at the venue.

More complicated to navigate was the political subtext to *Panjim 175*, which was mounted and opened during an especially contested and uneasy period in the city's relationship with its own administrators. Even while the exhibition was underway, I explained the context of this conundrum in "Coast to Coast" my weekly Times of India column, "An ugly surprise awaits visitors to Serendipity Arts Festival 2018 when they ascend the staircase to the immensely historic Adil Shah palace on the Panjim waterfront. One side of the sprawling first floor hosts superbly curated exhibitions by Rahaab Allana and Ranjit Hoskote. Those galleries brim full of spectacular images and artworks. But the rest of the space officially dedicated by the state to public cultural events is inexplicably closed off. It has been hijacked in plain sight by the perpetrators of Panjim's increasingly outrageous 'Smart City' scam."[14]

My column contended, "If civilisations can be defined by a single structure that is what the Adil Shah palace means to Goa. All that amazing history is traduced by the covert seizure of the historic monument, in the unforgivable absence of public consultation or meaningful oversight. All those glorious gallery spaces are now private domain. Excellent restoration of the building to global standards has been subverted, with air-conditioning ducts and vents punched into

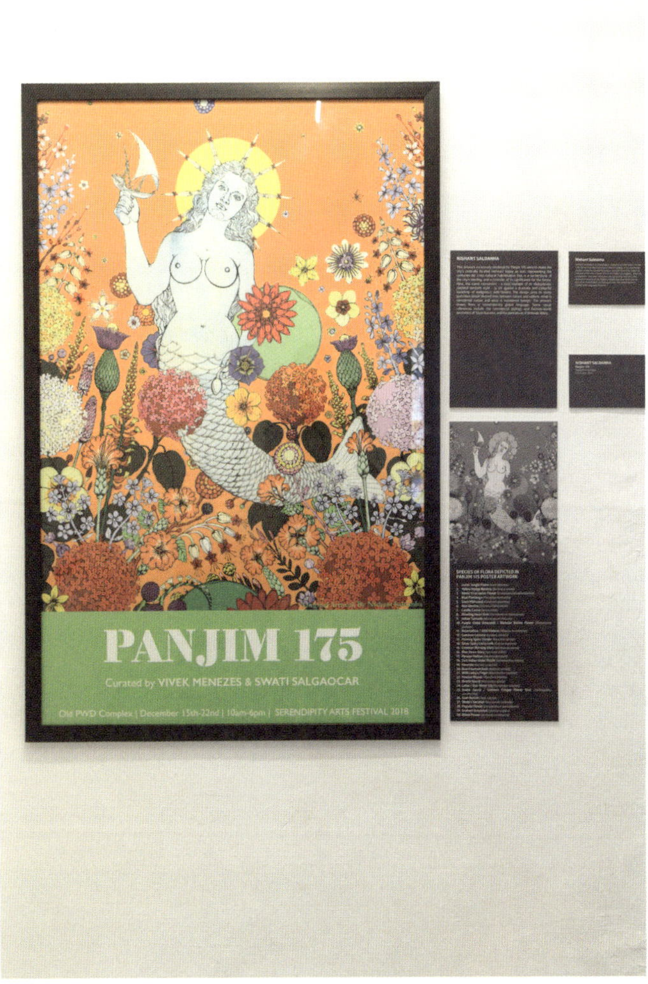

Poster made for *Panjim 175* (2018); Nishant Saldanha;
Digital Print; 21"x 28"

500-year-old walls. Bureaucrats twiddle thumbs under million-dollar lighting systems that were imported specifically for viewing artworks. Perhaps worst of all, the heist of one side of the top floor has rendered the exhibition spaces totally inaccessible to the disabled, elderly and wheel-chair bound. This is the extent of Panjim's 'smart city' farce."[15]

This was a self-conscious replay of *Aparanta*, which similarly addressed several disparate and equally important issues simultaneously. And just like that 2007 precedent, the "smart city scam" went national even while the exhibition was still underway. Mint, a national supplement quoted the Goan fashion designer Wendell Rodricks: "It was the vision of several iconic Goans like Mario Miranda and Charles Correa to use this heritage structure solely for art, art exhibitions and culture. This is a scandal and the offices must be thrown out."[16] One day later, the Goa Heritage Action Group raised its own voice about the occupation of the Old Secretariat, as well as the planned redevelopment of the "Obras Publicas" venue of *Panjim 175*, both of which had previously been pursued without public consultation or oversight.

Panjim 175 featured several artworks that were conceived in close collaboration with the artists, like Sonia Rodrigues Sabharwal's monumental series of paintings titled *Mystical Divine Grace: The Seven Sister Goddesses* (2018), representing the seven original sibling goddesses in Goa, which include the mind-bending "closest sisters" of Milagres (who is ostensibly Catholic) from Mapusa, and Lairai (who remains Hindu) from Shirgao, whose holy dwellings are only 15 kilometres apart. On the former's feast day, her sister sends the gift of coconuts, which are pressed to make oil used by pilgrims to anoint the Madonna statue (itself a very "Hindu" veneration). Very soon afterwards, the gifts go the other way, including wood that's used to make the fire-pit which devotees cross in bare feet to demonstrate their own fervour. Many Goans attend both events with equal sincerity.

The seven sisters were displayed surrounding another exclusive, commissioned artwork, a luminous glittering *roinn* or termite mound created by Waylon D'Souza titled *Roinn Reborn* (2018), which represented even older religious traditions linking Shantadurga (the iconic and unique Goan avatar of Durga where the goddess appears as harbinger of peace) to Santeri (the proto-Goddess of Goa's religious traditions, predating both Brahmanism and Christianity) and the indigenous religious practices that originated in this ancient territory.

Swati and I intended to consciously set aside the "great man" traditions of historiography and cultural representation, via radical inclusion of a multiplicity of voices, which have been muffled in Goan history. Some of these concerns were addressed by Pritha Sardessai, whose *Kapodanchi Kanni* (2018) installation of kunbi saris told the story of the territory's aboriginal weaving traditions, and Chaitali Morajkar, whose brilliant collage of paintings on text, *Swatantra* (2018) looked at the state's freedom struggle with a twist, by interviewing women who lived through those times and recording their hand-written testimonials of what the artist described as aspects of "freedom from different dimensions: political, domestic, and internal." Kausalya Gadekar's suite of works titled *The Sacred Synchrony* (2018) addressed the social exclusion of menstruating women, and Loretti Pinto's spectacular room-sized sculptural installation (including paintings and drawings) titled *Journey* (2018), addressed the bittersweet loss and longing engendered by migration.

Panjim 175 went beyond the formal "fine arts" spectrum and reached civil society organisations in the city. Thus, *The Bookworm Trust*, one of the leading children's literacy and library advocates in the country, created an astonishingly ambitious, interactive space along the Mandovi waterfront for its ongoing "Nhoi—The River Draw." And arrayed along the venue's courtyard were the Goa Bird Conservation Network with its display of bird-photographs, alongside rare original paintings by one of the world's consummate bird artists, the late Carl D'Silva (*Birds of the Indian Subcontinent*, 1998). The birders also curated an outstanding "soundtrack" of indigenous bird calls that played from the tree just outside their exhibition space, both confounding and delighting visitors all day long.

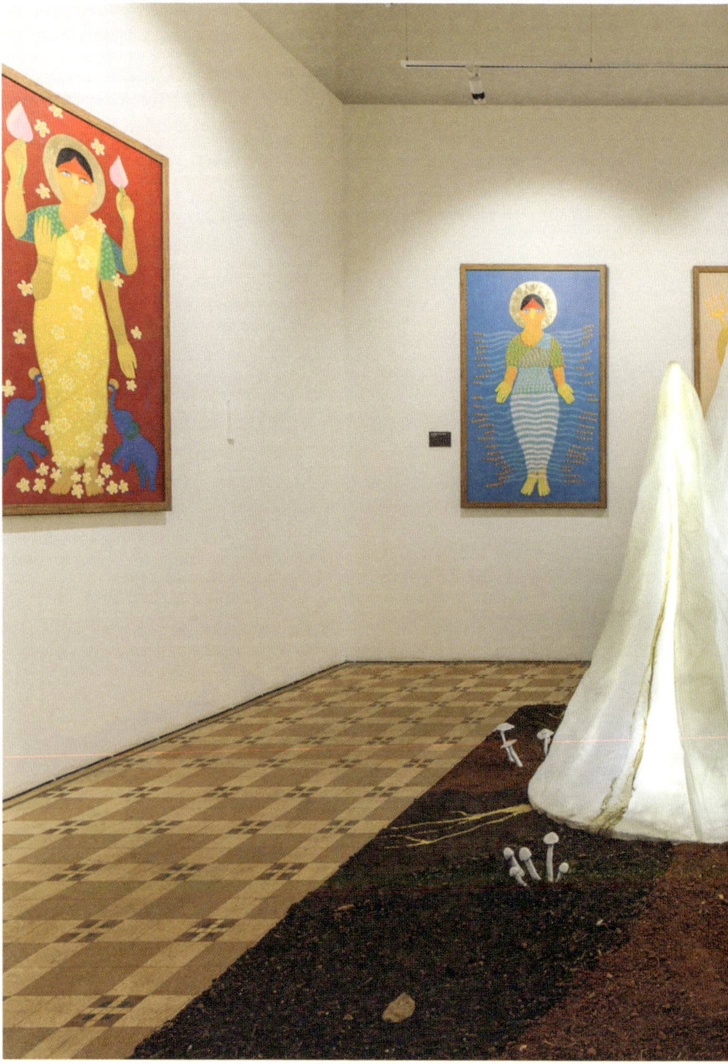

On the walls:
Mystical Divine Grace: The Seven Sister Goddesses (2018); Sonia Rodrigues Sabharwal; 5' x 3'

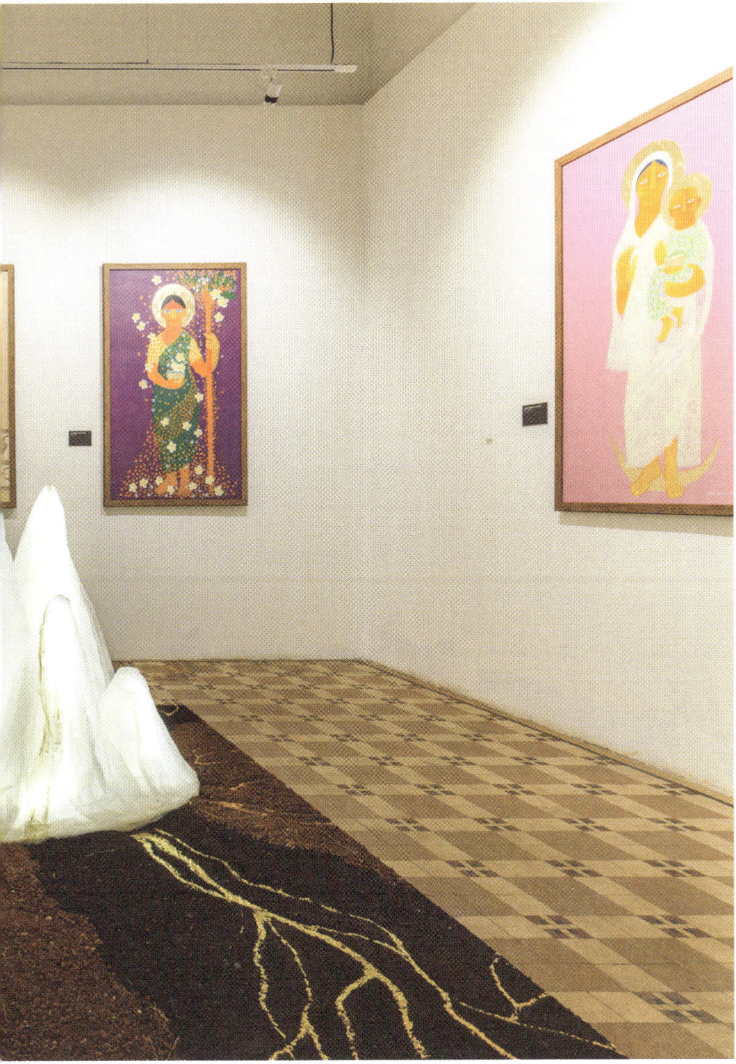

Centre of the room:
Roinn Reborn; Waylon D'Souza; Mixed waste, Organic material; 5' x 3' x 5'

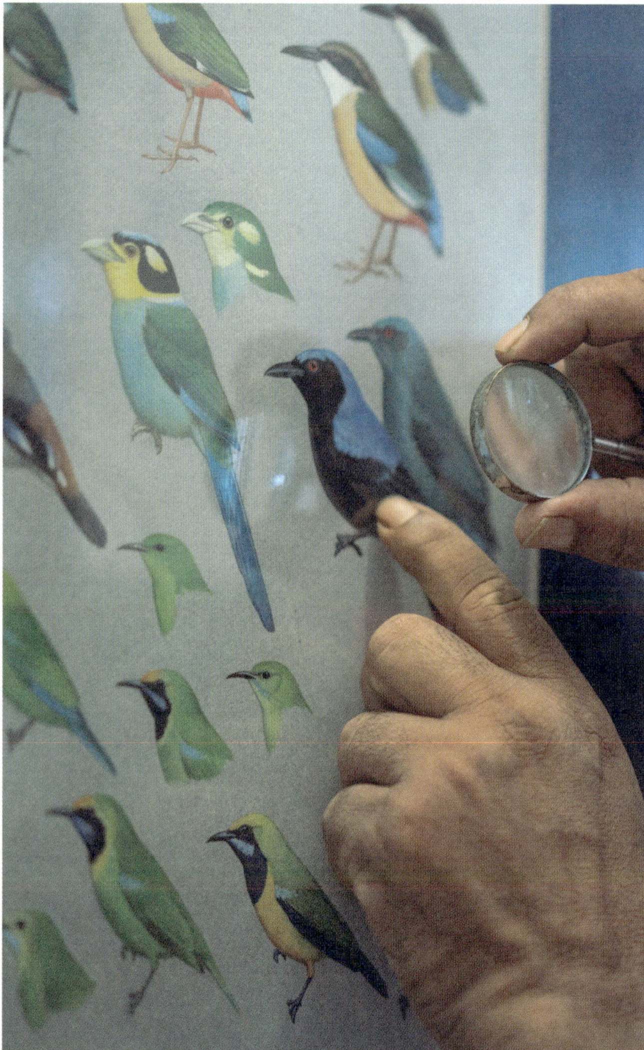

Birds of the Indian Subcontinent (1998); Carl D'Silva;
Colour Plates (watercolor on paper); Variable dimensions

Swati and I wanted people to wander into our venue but then to find good reason to pause there, hang on, spend extended time soaking in the art and atmosphere, and steadily open up to the delights of Panjim's quiet riverfront. To achieve that, we programmed micro-events extensively through the week. We each conducted two curated walks, which cumulatively witnessed the participation of over 500 visitors. We commissioned an exclusive suite of music from the pianist and conductor Parvesh Java, who paired Manoharrai Sardessai's Konkani classic for children *Bebeancho Kazar* (The Wedding of the Frogs) recited by the late poet's son and daughter-in-law, with eighteenth century Western classical music, to create an especially sublime moment.

There were five special lectures, including the inaugural Infosys lecture delivered by Professor Ananya Jahanara, titled "Rapsodia Ibero-Indiana: Transoceanic Goa and *The Musical World of Carlos Eugenio Ferreira* (1869–1932)"; Goa Heritage Action Group's Raya Shankhwalkar spoke on "Panjim: Heritage Conservation For a Smart City"; local-born star wildlife biologist Nandini Velho on "Art and Alliances for Conservation"; Goa College of Architecture's Vishvesh Kandolkar on "Rising From The Shadows of Old Goa: The Story of Panjim"; and separate presentations on the great Goan artists, Angelo da Fonseca (by Delio de Mendonça) and Francis Newton Souza (by Jugneeta Sudan). The beloved city theatre group Mustard Seeds also created and performed an exclusive production *Few Miles, Many Smiles* (2018). Most of these drew full houses, with the core audience returning to view it again, often commenting how they wished *Panjim 175* could continue permanently.

Over the course of the Serendipity Arts Festival, festival-goers first trickled and then poured into the old PWD complex in almost large numbers. We were particularly gladdened by the repeat visitors from Panjim, who lingered and luxuriated in this new public space with its unequalled access to the river. Many people signed up to support a spontaneous movement to preserve the buildings, and its waterfront. Simultaneously, another set of protests drew attention to the hijacking of the Old Secretariat. Meanwhile, our mermaid posters started popping up all over the city, and—via social media—on walls all over India and abroad. In the very last week of the year, it finally felt like justice had been done to the city's historic moment.

Notes

[1] Richard F. Burton, *Goa, and the Blue Mountains; Or, Six Months of Sick Leave* (Oxford: University of California Press, 1991), 22.

[2] Burton, *Goa, and the Blue Mountains; Or, Six Months of Sick Leave*, 27.

[3] Burton, *Goa, and the Blue Mountains; Or, Six Months of Sick Leave*, 102.

[4] Dane Kennedy, "Introduction," in *Goa and the Blue Mountains* by Richard F. Burton (Oxford: University of California Press, 1991), xii.

[5] Burton, *Goa, and the Blue Mountains*, 93.

[6] Burton, *Goa, and the Blue Mountains*, 94.

[7] Burton, *Goa, and the Blue Mountains*, 86.

[8] Sohini C, "Churchill's Real Darkest Hour: new evidence confirms British leader's role in murdering 3 million Bengalis," *South China Morning Post*, April 12 2019, URL: https://www.scmp.com/week-asia/opinion/article/3005838/churchills-real-darkest-hour-new-evidence-confirms-british

[9] Sohini C, "Churchill's Real Darkest Hour: new evidence confirms British leader's role in murdering 3 million Bengalis."

[10] Jawaharlal Nehru, "A Tryst with Destiny," published on *The Guardian: Great Speeches of 20th century*, May 1 2007, URL: https://www.theguardian.com/theguardian/2007/may/01/greatspeeches

[11] P. T. Reddy, *40 Years of P.T. Reddy's Art*, ed. A. S. Raman (Hyderabad: Andhra Pradesh Council of Artists, 1982), 29.

[12] Ranjit Hoskote, "Mapping the Invisible River: Contemporary Art in Goa," *Goanet Reader*, April 20, 2007, URL: http://lists.goanet.org/pipermail/goanet-news-goanet.org/2007-April/002037.html

[13] Hoskote, "Mapping the Invisible River: Contemporary Art in Goa."

[14] Vivek Menezes, "Daylight Robbery at Adil Shah Palace," *The Times of India*, December 17 2018, URL: https://timesofindia.indiatimes.com/city/goa/daylight-robbery-at-adil-shah-palace/articleshow/67119399.cms

[15] Menezes, "Daylight Robbery at Adil Shah Palace."

[16] Benita Fernando, "Goans oppose Smart City office in heritage palace," *LiveMint*, December 21 2018, URL: https://www.livemint.com/Politics/jVXbMCZRVTeNW7RDIuoeSP/Goans-oppose-Smart-City-office-in-heritage-palace.html

Biographies

Kamayani Sharma studied philosophy and gender studies at Fergusson College, Pune, and did her Master's from the School of Arts and Aesthetics, JNU. A former text editor with the Bombay-based visual arts quarterly ART India, Sharma is a regular contributor to Artforum, The Caravan and Scroll.in. Her writing has appeared in The White Review, Fulcrum: An Annual of Poetry & Aesthetics, The Kartika Review, Pratilipi, Take On Art, Firstpost and Studies in South Asian Film and Media. She has been a research associate to an anthropologist, taught philosophy to undergraduates, and is currently a researcher with the Delhi-based media studies programme, Sarai (CSDS).

Vivek Menezes is a widely published writer and photographer, and co-founder and co-curator of the acclaimed Goa Arts + Literature Festival.

About Projects/Processes

Projects/Processes is an initiative launched by Serendipity Arts Foundation in 2017 to publish commissioned research essays, longform writing, and in-depth criticism that explore the ideas and processes behind select curatorial projects at Serendipity Arts Festival. Over three years, the Festival has accumulated a rich database of creative energies and partnerships. As an eight-day long event, the Festival is a platform for multidisciplinary collaboration and cultural innovation, and has commissioned over 90 new works across the visual and performing arts since its inception in 2016. The Projects/Processes series offers an opportunity to give some of these works and the stories that they tell continued life, through a deeply engaged look at how they came together and their significance to the discourse of contemporary art in India moving forward. Each volume comprises essays covering distinct projects that stand in some dialogue with each other, through the questions they raise and the thematic landscape they cover.

Project Head & Editor: Senjuti Mukherjee
Managing Editor: Nandita Jaishankar
Copy editors: Arnav Adhikari & Arushi Vats
Cover design and layout: Aman Srivastava

Projects/Processes as an initiative is conceptualised and supported by Mr. S. K. Munjal, Founder Patron, Serendipity Arts Foundation and Ms. Smriti Rajgarhia, Director, Serendipity Arts Foundation.

About Serendipity Arts Festival

Serendipity Arts Festival (SAF) is one of the largest multi-disciplinary arts initiatives in the South Asian region. It spans the visual, performing and culinary arts, whilst exploring genres with film, live arts, literature and fashion. Besides the core content, which is conceptualised by an eminent curatorial panel, the Festival has various layers of programming, in the form of educational initiatives, workshops, special projects, and institutional engagements. Through active conversations between the artistic community and the urban, social landscape, the festival continues to evolve around the mandate of making art visible and accessible. The festival seeks collaborations at its core, inspiring new perspectives of seeing and experiencing. The Festival is a cultural experiment that also addresses issues such as arts education, patronage culture, interdisciplinary discourse, inclusivity and accessibility of the arts.

About Serendipity Arts Foundation

Serendipity Arts Foundation is an organisation that facilitates pluralistic cultural expressions, sparking conversations around the arts across the South Asian region. Committed to innovation and creativity, the aim of the Foundation is to support practice and research in the arts, as well as to promote sustainability and education in the field through a range of cultural and collaborative initiatives. The Foundation hosts projects through the year, which include institutional partnerships with artists and art organisations, educational initiatives, grants and outreach programmes across India.